The Predictability of Informal Conversation

THE PREDICTABILITY OF INFORMAL CONVERSATION

Christine Cheepen

Pinter Publishers London and New York

First published in Great Britain in 1988 by
Pinter Publishers Limited
25 Floral Street, London WC 2E 9DS

British Library Cataloguing in Publication Data
A CIP catalogue record for this book is available from the British Library

ISBN 0 86187 707 1

Typeset by Joshua Associates Ltd, Oxford
Printed by Biddles of Guildford Ltd.

Contents

Acknowledgements

Firstly, I would like to thank my parents, Peter and Mary Dare, for the encouragement, and the many kinds of support they have given me during the years which have led up to the completion of this work. I am also extremely grateful for the support of my husband, Dave, and my daughter, Lucy, who have helped me in so many practical ways, particularly in their heroic proof reading of the final manuscript.

For help with the content of this work I am indebted to a great many people; among them: John Wilson, of the University of Ulster, who was kind enough to let me argue with him by post early on in the work; George Turner, of the University of Adelaide, who has been extremely generous with his time, and has provided me with helpful and constructive criticism throughout all stages of composition—I only wish I had taken his advice in more areas; John Local, of the University of York, who arranged for me to have access to the Jefferson corpus; Fred Clark, of The Hatfield Polytechnic, who enabled me to collect the job interview tapes as part of my own corpus; Alan Hanslow of The Computer Centre, The Hatfield Polytechnic, to whom I am indebted for advice and help at various stages throughout the project; and my friends and relatives—particularly Cath and Celia—who were kind enough to forgive me for surreptitiously recording their conversations, and who have allowed me to use extracts of those tapes as examples in this work.

Finally, I wish to say a special thank you to my doctoral supervisor, Jim Monaghan, of The Hatfield Polytechnic. Throughout all stages of this work, he has provided thorough criticism and good advice—much of which I have been so foolish as to ignore. In addition to this, he has constantly given me encouragement, friendship, and great moral support whenever it has been needed—and he has done all this with grace, patience and great good humour. Thank you Jim—I owe you.

Christine Cheepen
The Hatfield Polytechnic, 1988

To Dave and Lucy

Introduction

For the past thirty years there has been an ongoing interest in the study of conversation, and scholars from various disciplines have contributed to the literature; apart from the mainstream research produced by linguists (see the subsequent chapters of this current work), scholars from other disciplines have also involved themselves—see, for example, the work of Stubbs and Bellack (education), Goffman and Argyle (sociology), and various writers involved in the field of psychoanalysis (in particular, Bateson's work on schizophrenia). Apart from the academic interest generated by the research, there have been a number of practical applications of the findings, but these have generally been restricted to the areas of EFL teaching in linguistics, classroom teaching and assessment in education, and some kinds of psycho-analytical therapy.

Today, however, in addition to the traditional interest in the complexities of human conversation, and the practical applications arising from that, there is an added dimension which affects almost all disciplines, and which has not only lent a new urgency to the academic interest in all kinds of conversation, but has also provided scope for a range of new practical applications.

This is the interest in dialogue which has arisen out of the computer revolution. Those who have, over the past few years, worked on producing the vast number of computer applications which operate in almost every walk of life, have, in most cases, had to contend with the problem of the 'front end'— the 'human/machine interface'. In many cases, this interface is adequately implemented in 'printed' form—i.e. printed messages on the screen—but an increasing need has emerged for spoken forms of human/machine interface, in order to cope with such developments as automatic answering systems and the many projects which need to take account of the problems of the disabled. Whether the implementation is to be in printed or spoken form, it is clear that this interface, to be successful, needs to be constructed with reference to the workings of human/human interface. A clear understanding of the structure of natural conversation is, then, now more important than it has ever been, as it must play a central role in the progress of the technological revolution, being very much a part of the 'front end' of the many areas in which computer systems operate.

Because certain aspects of conversation have proved to be so elusive to the analyst, much work has been left undone. Informal, spontaneous conversation in particular has posed many problems for the analyst/writer attempting to provide a rigorous description of the phenomenon, and yet it is clear to all researchers in the field (and indeed to anyone who considers the matter at all) that it is of paramount importance to the study of all kinds of conversation, as it is essentially the stuff from which the more formal, stereotyped (and therefore more easily analysable) kinds of conversation are built.

For this reason, this work is primarily a study of informal, spontaneous conversation—though other, more formal kinds of conversation (interviews, tutorials) are discussed and analysed, in order to set the main discussion in some kind of context. The analysis reveals a previously unrecognised patterning in informal conversation (which is paralleled by a similar patterning in the formal kinds of conversation) and a strong predictability arising out of that patterning, which will be of interest not only to those concerned with the study of conversation for its own sake, but also to those involved in the construction of the automatic systems which attempt to simulate natural conversation.

0.1 Theoretical context

Linguistics is a necessary part of the study of people in their environment; and their environment consists, first and foremost, of other people.

[Halliday 1975: 17]

It is widely recognised that communication between speakers in dialogue is a multi-stranded phenomenon, involving the exchange of various kinds of meaning simultaneously, though writers do not agree on the precise distinctions which should be made between these strands.

Buhler (1934), for instance, presents a tripartite model of 'representation', 'expression' and 'vocative' (redefined as 'referential', 'emotive' and 'conative' by Jakobson in his development and extension of the model in 1960); and Lyons (1977), refers to 'three more or less distinguishable functions: the descriptive, the social and the expressive'. Halliday (1973) uses the term 'ideational' to refer to the aspect of meaning which Lyons terms 'descriptive', but includes 'social' and 'expressive' in his category of 'interpersonal', and adds a further strand—'textual' meaning.

While acknowledging that different strands of communication are indeed present in any speech encounter, there has been a general tendency among linguists dealing with discourse of all types to focus primarily on the

IDEATIONAL or DESCRIPTIVE strand of meaning—which is seen as the carrier of information about the world—and, therefore, the carrier of topic in discourse—and the TEXTUAL, which organises the structure of the discourse. The interpersonal strand has been viewed generally as operating primarily at the micro-level of the utterance, so that its importance for the discourse as a whole has been ignored. It is this neglected aspect of the interpersonal strand of communication which is the focus of the following chapters.

It will become clear, as the argument and exemplification proceeds throughout the succeeding chapters, that the interpersonal strand is important in two major ways. Firstly, the establishment and monitoring of an appropriate interpersonal framework account for much of the linguistic work done by speakers. Secondly (and more importantly), the interpersonal component is, in fact, the basis on which other strands of meaning are built. Throughout the remainder of this work I shall show how the interpersonal strand is crucial to spoken discourse of various types, and examples will be given to support the claims made. Finally, I shall summarise the points which have been made throughout the work, and reassess the relationships between the 'ideational', 'interpersonal' and 'textual' strands in various kinds of discourse.

In order to achieve this end, it is first necessary to look more closely at what constitutes the interpersonal strand—what we might recognise as the characteristic elements of communication at the purely interpersonal level of discourse. I suggest that there are two inter-related general concepts which are important here, and which between them cover all aspects of spoken interpersonal communication; they are DISCOURSE GOAL and RELATIVE SPEAKER STATUS, both of which will be discussed in more detail in sections 0.2 and 0.3 immediately following.

0.2 Goal as a determining factor in speech encounters

Speech encounters can be seen as falling into two basic categories, depending on the kind of goal which predominates, whether that goal be internal or external to the encounter.

A goal which is external to the encounter is one which is concerned with having an effect of some kind on the 'outside' world (i.e. getting one or more of the participants of the encounter to perform some action, take on some particular responsibility, change the world in some way).

An 'internal' goal is not be found outside the encounter—it is not a matter of achieving an effect on the world—it is, rather, a matter of achieving some kind of effect on the 'inner' shared world of the participants of the encounter—the INTERPERSONAL world, or the relationship between speaker and hearer as operating through a particular encounter.

To discuss these two different kinds of goal, and the kinds of encounters associated with them, I shall, throughout this work, refer to 'transactional' (i.e. external goal), and 'interactional'—or 'interactive'—(i.e. internal goal). Both these terms are borrowed from Brown and Yule: 'interactional language is primarily LISTENER ORIENTED, whereas transactional language is primarily MESSAGE ORIENTED' (1983: 13), the nature of 'message' being strongly bound to actions or events in the world outside the encounter, rather than aspects of speaker/hearer relationship within the encounter. What I refer to as 'transactional' language can, of course, be described as the kind of language where the 'ideational' strand is prominent compared with the interpersonal. I shall, however, continue to use the term 'transactional', firstly because it contrasts appropriately with the term 'interactional', and secondly because 'ideational', 'interpersonal' and 'textual' are terms which relate only to LINGUISTIC categories WITHIN A TEXT. 'Transactional' and 'interactional', on the other hand, are terms which relate both to the text and to the wider concept of linguistic activity in a text as an instance of human social behaviour, and which lend themselves more readily to association with discourse goals as a subset of social goals. More detailed comments on transactional and interactional goals will follow in Chapter 2.

0.3 Status as a framework for speech encounters

Within any speech encounter, whether transactional or interactional, the co-conversationalists will adopt an interpersonal orientation towards one another, in terms of their relative status, so that they will adopt complementary roles of superior/inferior, or equal/equal.

A major claim of this work is that the status patterns which are adopted in dialogue are an important aspect of both transactional and interactional encounters in that they serve to define the precise nature of the encounter, and to enable the participants to pursue their goal, whether that goal be transactional or interactional. As Thomas, writing about unequal encounters, in 'The Language of Power' says: 'the power relationship obtaining between the participants in an interaction and the institutional norms within which that interaction takes place are central to the way in which the discourse is developed' (1985: 766). While I shall discuss examples of unequal encounters in this work (I use the term 'fixed status' encounters, see section 2.3. in Chapter 2), I am primarily concerned with what are, in general terms, encounters between EQUAL participants ('variable status' encounters, see section 2.4, Chapter 2), and I shall show that status is not only important in unequal encounters; it is also a crucial element in spoken discourse between equals, my examples being drawn from friendly chats between intimates.

The following chapters, which will be concerned with showing that this claim is justified, will deal with the various ways in which status can be seen to operate in dialogue.

A distinction will be made between 'fixed status' encounters (i.e. those in which the transactional goal is paramount) and 'variable status' encounters (those in which the interactional goal is paramount), and subsequent chapters will draw on this distinction in order to discuss the ways in which status is signalled and used to progress the discourse in both transactional and interactional dialogue.

The major part of the work will be concerned with the analysis of primarily interactional encounters, and the examples and discussion will show that:

1. they have a special communication structure for the progress of topics;
2. that this communication structure is such as to allow status to be continually adjusted throughout the encounter;
3. that unadjusted movements or variations of status in interactional encounters call up special speaker tactics which result in topic change and topic movement over large sections of the discourse.

In pursuance of these aims, and bearing in mind my intention to focus mainly on interactional encounters, six areas will be covered.

Chapter 1 will deal with an overview of the work done by other writers who have been concerned with the study of discourse—particularly those who have commented on the area of primarily interactional encounters—and will discuss the usefulness of the various approaches.

Chapter 2 will discuss goal and status and the general ways in which these factors operate in transactional and interactional encounters.

Chapter 3 will deal with the signalling and operation of status in transactional encounters, and will relate the findings of this work to that done on other types of fixed status encounters such as classroom discourse.

Chapter 4 will present a new model of interactional discourse—a model which provides for the introduction and progress of topics, while taking account of status considerations.

Chapter 5 will show how, within an interactional encounter, status patterns may alter and become unacceptable to participants. It will then describe how speakers deal with such situations, the special tactics they employ to rebuild an acceptable status pattern, and the effects these tactics have on topic change and topic movement over large sections of the discourse.

Chapter 6, drawing conclusions from the findings of the previous chapters, will show how status, the interactive level of communication, and topic management are related, and what this means in terms of the concepts 'ideational', 'interpersonal' and 'textual', and will also make suggestions regarding potential future directions for research in the same field.

0.4 Nature and function of the data

The general data on which the arguments in this work are based are the various forms of language which I, as a native speaker of English, recognise as being used in the multiplicity of speech situations which arise within British society—particularly that which I have observed during the preparation of this work in the past three years.

Where examples are given to illustrate certain points, these are, in the main, taken from the corpus of dialogic encounters which I have collected, studied and analysed, as part of this current work (approximately 40,000 words). I have made a similar study of two other corpora (which are also referred to for exemplification in subsequent chapters): the dialogic content of the London–Lund Corpus, which is held by the Survey of English Usage, University College, London (approximately 340,000 words); and a corpus of telephone dialogues collected by Gail Jefferson (approximately 60,000 words), which is held at the University of York. The comments I make throughout this work, though focusing mainly on my own corpus, are supported by the evidence in these secondary sources. All examples are from genuine conversational encounters—none was constructed to prove a point, and all passages cited are selected from similar material massively present in the data (both my own and the other two corpora).

My own corpus consists of eight conversations which fall into three categories:

1. DRESSES, XMAS 83, CELIA, DAWSONS, JOHN. These are all primarily interactional conversations; DRESSES, XMAS 83 and CELIA are all two-party 'coffee cup' chats between women in their mid- to late thirties who are, in the case of the first two, close friends, and in the case of the last one, closely related. DAWSONS is a five-party conversation between a married couple, Geoff and Chris, and a family at whose home they are spending a social evening—Jack, Catherine and their ten-year-old daughter, Mary. Jack and Geoff are friends and have business connections, Catherine and Chris have met once before, and Mary, the child, is previously unacquainted with Geoff and Chris, the visitors. JOHN is a conversation between a brother and sister-in-law, both in their late thirties, who are well acquainted, but have not met for several months.

All these conversations were recorded as surreptitiously as possible. That is, although I was actually a participant in all of them, I was the only participant in each case who was aware that the conversation was being recorded—the other participants in each case were only informed of the recording at a later date.

There could, of course, be an objection to the reliability of the evidence in these tapes, based on the fact that I was a participant and could, theoretically, have deliberately guided the various conversations in order to produce certain effects. In practice, however, this would not, under the circumstances, be possible, as would be recognised by anyone who had attempted a similar project. In conversations such as those I recorded, the speaker(s) who is unaware of being recorded speaks and reacts, of course, absolutely naturally, which pressurises the speaker who is aware of being recorded to respond equally naturally, and even, as the conversation proceeds, to initiate topics, interrupt and at times take control of the discourse without adjusting his/her linguistic behaviour in any way to take account of the recording. Any unnaturalness on the part of that speaker would be noticed and (in a relaxed conversation between intimates, which these conversations are), remarked upon, so that, sooner or later, the unaware speaker would be likely to make an overt reference to the 'oddness' of his/her co-conversationalist, e.g. *what's up with you*, *are you OK*, *what are you up to*, or even *oh God, you're not taping this are you*. None of the tapes contains any such comment, and are all clearly 'real' conversations.

One way to avoid even the suspicion that the taped conversations could have somehow been deliberately 'managed' would have been to record people talking while I was not present, so that the recordings would have truly been surreptitious, but I rejected this idea as it seemed to me both unethical and potentially very damaging to my own continuing relationships with the speakers; as Chapter 5 shows, people who are known to co-conversationalists but absent from the encounter can, on occasions, be the subject of the most ferocious kind of criticism. The conversations in the other two corpora which provide additional examples were also recorded under similar conditions of semi-surreptitiousness, and these too are clearly ordinary, spontaneous conversations.

2. KEYTE and GILBEY. These are both audio tracks from video tapes made of job interviews. They are not, in fact, 'real' job interviews, because, in each case, the job apparently on offer is not actually vacant. The interviews were conducted as part of a two-day interviewing course for employees of Hertfordshire County Council, which is run several times each year at The Hatfield Polytechnic. The procedure for this part of the course is to prepare for and conduct an interview for a job which does actually exist within the County Council; those employees who are on the course at the time are divided into groups and must act as an interviewing panel—the 'interviewees' (of whom I was one) are individuals who are known to the lecturers who run the course but not to those who are to act as 'interviewers'. The aim of the exercise is to make the interview as realistic as possible—for instance, the interviewee must fill out an application form in advance, and is questioned by the panel largely on the information provided on that form. All interviews are recorded on video tape, so that the 'interviewers' can assess their own individual and collective performance later, and can thereby improve their

interviewing techniques in 'real life' situations. There is, of course, a degree of stress in the performance for all participants, occasioned by the presence of video cameras and the knowledge that not only the 'interviewee' but also the 'interviewers' are on some kind of trial. This stress is, however, constant for all participants, so that, although it may sometimes cause the participants to behave in a more formal manner than would be the case in a real interview, it does not result in any kind of skewing in the interaction between interviewee and interviewers, and, as the examples which are used throughout this work show, the result appears to be a completely believable job interview.

3. JULIE. This is a taped tutorial between a lecturer at The Hatfield Polytechnic and a second-year degree student. It was recorded in similar conditions to the primarily interactional conversations—DRESSES, XMAS 83, CELIA, DAWSONS and JOHN—in that the tutor was aware that the conversation was being recorded, while the student was not. Again, it is clear from listening to the tape, and from inspection of the extracts used in this work, that the tutor's awareness of being recorded in no way caused him to behave or speak unnaturally.

Transcription conventions

Speakers in some transcriptions are referred to by initials, rather than names; this is in the interests of anonymity.

Pauses are indicated by . (short pause) and - (longer pause, one second approx.).

Overlapping speech is indicated by * * and by + +. Two sets of symbols have been used for this indication in order to avoid confusion in cases where two sets of overlapping speech may themselves overlap, as in:

> *hello*
> he*llo +how* are you+
> +nice to see you+

N.B. The London–Lund Corpus occasionally, in cases of multiple over-lapping, uses a double symbol: ** **.

London–Lund: Examples have been copied as they appear in the original corpus, but intonation markings have been omitted.

Jefferson: Examples have been copied as they appear in the original corpus.

1 Some approaches to interactional encounters

What I have referred to as 'primarily interactional encounters' have been described elsewhere as 'casual, spontaneous conversation', and this has been dealt with by a number of writers, who have commented on some of the characteristics of such dialogues from a grammatical and stylistic viewpoint. The sort of items which have been noted (for instance, by Crystal and Davy 1969, 1975) are loose co-ordination of clauses, frequency of minor sentences, phrasal verbs, informal 'filler' verbs, contracted verbal forms such as *he's*, *I'll* etc.

While such observations are demonstrably true, they are not helpful to an understanding of the interactional workings of the encounter, and the connections it may have with topic movement and management. With regard to topic management, Crystal and Davy state that informal, spontaneous conversation is characterised by:

randomness of the subject matter ... the absence of any conscious planning as conversation proceeds. Conversation does not take place in a series of coordinated blocks, but—especially as someone searches for the beginning of a topic—in a series of jumps ... There is a general absence of linguistic or cultural pressures to make the conversation go in a particular direction. [1969: 115]

This is a view shared by a number of other writers, notably Sinclair and Coulthard, who state: 'In normal conversation ... changes of topic are unpredictable' (1975: 4)

An important claim of this current work is that topic and topic movement in interaction are not simply a chance affair, as suggested by the above quotes. This is not to suggest that the succession of topics is prepared in advance by speakers, nor that the occurrence of particular topics can be predicted. It will be shown, in Chapter 4, that topics are raised and discussed in particular ways, and arise largely out of particular elements in the discourse, which form part of the interactive basis of the dialogue; and, as Chapter 5 will demonstrate, there are occasions when it is possible to predict that topic change WILL occur, and also the DIRECTION (chronologically speaking) which it will take.

As to the transactional encounters studied in this work, there is some slight indication in the interview tapes (KEYTE and GILBEY) that a particular kind of topic is likely to RECUR in job interviews (see Chapter 3, section 3.1.1 Examples 2 and 5), but a considerably larger sample of transactional material would have to be amassed in order to establish the general predictability of this, a task which is outside the scope of this current work.

1.1 Discourse management and topical goal

The writers most prominent in this area of interactional encounters are the group generally known as the ethnomethodologists (Sacks, Schegloff, Jefferson, etc.), who, having their academic background in sociology rather than linguistics, take a completely different view of casual, spontaneous conversation from other writers. They do not comment on the various grammatical structures which tend to characterise this kind of discourse—they deal, instead, with the MANAGEMENT of the whole encounter, taking into account factors such as who speaks when, placement of topics, and progression towards, and digression from particular topical goals. The way speakers organise 'who speaks when' is by a turn-taking system, which is composed of a 'turn constructional component', a 'turn allocational component' and a set of rules which cover both the construction and the allocation of turns (a detailed description of this system can be found in Schenkein 1978).

As a substantial part of this study is concerned with the kinds of conversational turns which may be taken in discourse, and the relationship of particular kinds of turns to topic movement, it will be helpful now, and relevant to my discussion, to outline the way in which the ethnomethodologists account for the placement of topics, and progression towards (and digression from) particular topical goals.

1.1.1 Placement of topics

The observations of the ethnomethodologists have shown that placement is crucial to the organisation and understanding of dialogue. This is illustrated in the discussion of 'adjacency pairs' (Schegloff and Sacks, in Turner 1974: 238), where the authors point out the interdependence of two-part units of dialogue, such as question/answer and summons/answer, and show that just as the occurrence of a 'first part' of such a pair will, in some way, define what comes next as the appropriate 'second part', so the uttering of that second part in a similar way helps to define what precedes it as the appropriate first part:

Past and current work has indicated that placement considerations are general for utterances. That is: a pervasively relevant issue (for participants) about utterances in conversation is 'why that now' . . . some utterances may derive their character as actions entirely from placement considerations. For example, there do not seem to be criteria other than placement (i.e. sequential) ones that will sufficiently discriminate the status of an utterance as a 'statement', 'assertion', 'declarative', 'proposition', etc., from its status as an 'answer' . . . Finding an utterance to be an 'answer' [can only be accomplished] by consulting its sequential placement [1974: 241–2]

The notion of placement being of crucial importance to participants' understanding of dialogue is carried through to the management of topic throughout conversation. Schegloff and Sacks discuss the phenomenon of 'first topic' (1974: 243), which they describe as 'the reason for' the conversation (from the point of view of the participants). They also point out that speakers frequently decide to place 'first topic' somewhere other than first (chronologically) in the conversation. This is due to the tendency of speakers to place topics as though they arise 'naturally' from other topics which have already been discussed:

A feature of the organisation of topic talk seems to involve 'fitting' as a preferred procedure. That involves holding off the mention of a mentionable until it can 'occur naturally', that is, until it can be fitted to another conversationalist's prior utterance, allowing his utterance to serve as a sufficient source for the mentioning of the mentionable (thereby achieving a solution to the placement question, 'why that now' [1974: 243]

The notions of 'fitting', and suitable 'placement' of topics are highly relevant to my discussion of the interactive level of communication, though my approach differs substantially from that of the ethnomethodologists. These points will be dealt with in detail in Chapters 3, 4 and 5.

1.1.2 Progression towards and digression from topical goal

Most of the work in this area has been done by Jefferson, who discusses, at some length, 'side sequences' (in Sudnow, 1972: 294–338).

As the term implies, a 'side sequence' is a digression from the current topical goal of the conversation, a sequence of utterances which interrupts the main flow of the conversation, and after which participants return to that main, topical flow. Jefferson discusses side sequences primarily in connection with what she refers to as 'repairs' to the conversation.

The notions of both 'side sequence' and 'repair' are based, of course, on the assumption that the conversation is, in fact, 'going somewhere', topically speaking—that speakers are, indeed, progressing, step by step, through a particular topic to its agreed end, and that they 'interrupt' their progression on this path to effect a 'repair' by means of a 'side sequence', in order to clear obstacles out of the way.

These observations by Jefferson contradict the view taken by Crystal and Davy and by Sinclair and Coulthard that casual conversation is characterised by a lack of topical organisation, and Jefferson's views are supported by my evidence, and the discussion thereof found in the following chapters. I would add, however, that Jefferson's work (and that of all the ethnomethodologists), while showing great insight into the PRACTICAL workings and management of conversation, does not take account of its INTERACTIONAL workings and management, and it is this interactional level which is the focus of this current work. Chapter 5 will give a detailed explanation of the difference between PRACTICAL management (which applies equally to both interactional and transactional encounters) and INTERACTIONAL management, and will exemplify the relationship between the practical management of dialogue—i.e. manipulation of the turn taking system—and interactionally governed topic movement.

1.2 Interactional encounters and classroom discourse

Encounters which are primarily interactional have been discussed in passing in the work of a number of writers whose main area of study has been fixed-status, transactional encounters, and there has been a general tendency to assume that a close and detailed analysis of such fixed status encounters will ultimately provide some basis for the more daunting task of analysing casual, spontaneous (variable status) encounters. For example, much of the work of Sinclair and Coulthard (of the Birmingham school) has been concerned primarily with classroom discourse, and, in *Towards an Analysis of Discourse* (1975) Sinclair and Coulthard clearly indicate that the model they propose is not designed to deal with casual conversation. Burton, however, in 1980, does use the system proposed by Sinclair and Coulthard in her analysis of just this kind of discourse, although, in order to make the analysis workable, she begins by making certain modifications to the basic model.

The Sinclair and Coulthard model is a rank scale, consisting of a hierarchy of elements—Act, Move, Exchange, Transaction and Lesson—and the major modifications suggested by Burton are to the concept of 'move', which appears to be the element most crucial to the system.

The really interesting interactive ranks are those of Exchange and Move. And since the description of Exchange structure hinges on what Moves are used in what orders and relationships, and since Move is also the minimum interactive unit, it seems that most analytical problems centre on this rank first and foremost. [Burton 1980: 140]

(N.B. Burton's use of the term 'interactive' here is not to be understood in the same way as my use of the term; for Burton (and all the Birmingham school) 'interaction' is equivalent to what I call 'encounter'.)

The original model proposed by Sinclair and Coulthard sets up five classes of Move—Framing, Focusing, Opening, Answering and Follow-up; these are, of course, designed to deal with the analysis of classroom discourse, and are, therefore, not the most suitable categories for the analysis of casual conversation.

Burton proposes seven classes of Move—Framing, Focusing, Opening, Supporting, Challenging, Bound Opening, and Re-opening. I shall discuss only two of these—Supporting and Challenging—in more detail here, as a further explanation of the way Burton views these categories will be sufficient to illustrate the way in which her analysis of casual conversation differs from the approach I am taking in this current work.

Burton's use of the terms 'Supporting' and 'Challenging' does not relate to variations in the relationship of the speakers; it relates, rather, to preceding sections in the TEXT: 'The idea in general is that in casual conversation speakers can Support a previous piece of TEXT rather than a previous speaker' (Burton 1980: 150). This puts her approach very much in line with that taken by Longacre (1983, Chapter 2), who refers to 'Resolving' or 'Continuing Utterances', which progress or redirect the ongoing talk in the same way as Burton's Supporting or Challenging Moves.

Burton explains (1980: 150), that:

As Supporting Moves function to facilitate the topic presented in a previous utterance, or to facilitate the contribution of a topic implied in a previous utterance, Challenging Moves function to hold up the progress of that topic or topic-introduction in some way.

Supporting Moves, then, continue the direction of talk begun by the previous Move, whereas Challenging Moves in some way change that direction, and as Burton comments (151): 'although I have chosen the mnemonic "Challenge", I certainly do not intend it necessarily to indicate hostility. A Challenging Move may divert the ongoing talk in quite an amicable way'.

She does, however, point out that there are different kinds of Challenging Move, some of which appear, in fact, to operate as a challenge to the previous SPEAKER, and this can result in the opening of a new 'Transaction' (which Burton equates roughly with the introduction of a new topic):

a Challenging Move can be made by supplying an unexpected and inappropriate Act where the expectation of another has been set up . . . At its most extreme, of course, this type of Challenge filters upwards through the system and brings about the opening of a new Transaction. [151]

This brief comment does reveal some awareness of possible links between Challenges (in the sense of interactional trouble between speakers) and topic shift, but Burton does not pursue this line of thought. Chapter 5 will show that, when speaker Challenges are prolonged, they not only lead to topic shift—they lead, in many cases, to the introduction of a particular type of new topic (see Chapter 5, section 5.2.5, for discussion of 'scapegoat repairs'), and this new topic itself is followed by another shift, which involves a chrono-logical move 'backwards' in the conversation (see section 5.2.5.1.1 for discussion of 'topic loops').

The non-hostile Challenges mentioned by Burton involve clarificatory sequences, and are very similar to the 'Counter Questions' described by Longacre (1983: 51) which lead, in Longacre's terminology, to 'Abeyance Repartee', and to the 'repairs', which Jefferson discusses (in Sudnow, 1972), and which initiate 'side sequences' (already discussed in section 1.1.2 above).

The same phenomenon of sequences of clarification is, then, observed and discussed, under different names, by Burton, Longacre and Jefferson. All these writers, however, take the view that these sequences function to 'help' the ongoing flow of the current topic of talk, and that, after such a sequence, the speakers return to the 'mainstream' of the conversation. Such cases do, of course, occur in dialogue, but it is not always so; subsequent discussion and exemplification will show that clarificatory sequences can be used in dialogue in order to provide a suitable topical place for an otherwise unmentionable comment. In other words, the clarificatory sequence can be used to answer (in advance) the question of 'why that now?' Burton's approach, then, like the rest of the Birmingham school, is concerned (as is that of the ethnomethodo-logists) with the PRACTICAL workings of conversation, in terms of local discourse management and organisation.

1.3 Interactional encounters and phatic communion

I shall, in subsequent chapters of this work, use the word 'chat' to refer to a particular kind of dialogue in which the interactional aspect is paramount; an earlier (more impressive) term was coined by Malinowski, to refer to such talk, 'phatic communion' (1923: 315). I have, till now, avoided using this term, not because it is inappropriate in any way, but because, since 1923, it has been used by a number of writers other than Malinowski to refer to kinds of speech other than that originally specified by Malinowski, and its meaning has, in fact, been greatly restricted by these other writers. I shall now summarise the points made by Malinowski on this subject in 1923, and give a brief account of how his original definition has since been reinterpreted.

1.3.1 Malinowski and language as a mode of behaviour

Malinowski's comments on phatic communion are best understood in the light of what he has to say about language in general.

In his study of meaning in 'primitive languages' he divides language functions into two basic categories: 'language as a means of thinking', in which he includes 'poetic and literary production' and 'works of science and philosophy', involving 'certain very special uses' of language, and 'highly developed types of speech', all of which he refers to as a 'far-fetched and derivative function of language' (1923: 312); and 'language as a mode of action' (312), which includes all other language functions.

'Language as a mode of action' is sub-divided into three major function types:

1. Speech-in-action.
This is the kind of speech used 'in connection with vital work' (312), that is, the utterances are 'embedded in action', and function as 'a link in concerted human activity'. (N.B. The kind of activity observed by Malinowski in his field study in the Trobriand Islands, and referred to by him as involving Speech-in-action, is a fishing expedition, a clear example of 'vital work', needing 'concerted human activity'. The kind of speech encounters which provide the examples for this study do not involve this kind of language use, but I shall deal with this point in more detail in Chapter 4, section 4.1.2.)

Clearly, this kind of speech involves instructions, commands, warnings, and the like, all of which may be issued to facilitate the ongoing action. It also, however, according to Malinowski, includes speech which does not facilitate action, but is totally dependent on it, such as utterances expressing: 'keenness in the pursuit or impatience at some technical difficulty, joy of achievement or disappointment at failure' (1923: 311).

2. Free narrative
This type also has links with action, but, as Malinowski points out (313), 'it refers to action only indirectly'. Unlike the other function types, it has connections with two situations, the current speech situation of TELLING the narrative, and the situation in which the narrative is set which is separated from the current (narrative telling) situation in time.

It is worth noting here that, among the Trobriand Islanders at the time of Malinowski's study, free narrative was an institutionalised form of entertainment, told by one narrator for the benefit of an audience. In subsequent chapters of this work I shall show that, in chats, speakers spend much of their time telling stories. These are collaborative stories, in which both speakers contribute to the telling, so that the form of dialogue is preserved; stories are not, therefore, instances of free narrative (although examples of free narrative can still be found in modern society), in which one speaker has the right and duty to tell the story, and the other speaker(s) has the right and duty to act as the audience.

3. Phatic communion
This is a function type which, unlike Speech-in-action and free narrative, is unconnected with concerted human activity. It is, as Malinowski says:

'deprived of any context of situation' (313), because the meaning of utterances performing this function seems to be independent of any action which they may, by chance, accompany. He refers to it (ibid.) as 'the language used in free, aimless social intercourse' which occurs when people are relaxing, or when they are accompanying 'some mere manual work by gossip quite unconnected with what they are doing'.

Such language does not, then, have any kind of goal comparable to that of Speech-in-action (the kind of goal I have referred to as 'transactional'). The goal of phatic communion is the establishment and maintenance of social bonds between the speakers: 'Each utterance is an act serving the direct aim of binding hearer to speaker by a tie of some social sentiment or other' (315).

In addition to this general definition and description of phatic communion, Malinowski gives a number of suggestions as to how this may be realised in speech, such as: 'formulae of greeting or approach', 'comments on what is perfectly obvious', 'pure sociabilities'. It is, perhaps, these comments which have led later writers to reinterpret Malinowski's original definition.

1.4 Phatic communion reinterpreted

Since Malinowski, a number of linguists have referred to 'phatic communion' or the phatic use of language, but it is interesting to note that they have, in the main, departed from Malinowski's original definition, where his intention was clearly to include not only the short phatic phases which might occur at the beginning of, and perhaps during conversations, but also (perhaps primarily) to include lengthy stretches of chat, lasting perhaps for several hours.

There are two major views of phatic communion which appear to recur throughout the literature—its 'ice-breaking' function and its 'meaningless-ness'.

The 'ice-breaking' view of phatic communion appears to originate from Malinowski's 1923 comment that: 'to a natural man, another man's silence is not a reassuring factor, but, on the contrary, something alarming and dangerous' (314). The 'meaningless' view also has its foundation in Malinowski's original comments: 'A mere phrase of politeness, in use as much among savage tribes as in a European drawing room, fulfils a function to which the meaning of its words is almost completely irrelevant' (1923: 313).

Both these widely held views support a general consensus that phatic communion is, by definition, non-hostile. Simpson, in his 1986 article (Harris, Little and Singleton 1986), bases his discussion of phatic communion on what I regard as the very narrow and restricted view that phatic exchanges have a communicative function only in so far as they 'serve to break any uncomfortable silence as well as laying the foundation for further interaction' (233). He comments (p. 237) that: 'the most important motivation behind phatic initiation is that the speaker wants to declare that his intentions are pacific', and sums up (and thereby redefines) phatic exchanges as 'politeness strategies' (239). This view has been almost universal among writers who have approached the study of phatic communion, and it has, therefore, come to be understood as a type of speech which is inoffensive and uncontroversial: 'if you say "The nights are getting longer these days, aren't they", no one can possibly disagree with you' (Leech 1974: 62). This very inoffensiveness leads to the view, also expressed by Leech (ibid.), that phatic communion is 'dull and pedestrian'. At no point does Leech (or the majority of other writers) account for the possibility of different kinds of social contact, different qualities of social interaction. For Leech, the function of phatic communion is to promote and maintain 'the equilibrium of society' (62), it takes the form of inoffensive, uncontroversial remarks, it is 'dull and pedestrian', and: 'so long as a conversational hiatus is filled, what one says matters little' (62).

In his 1983 work, Leech again refers (briefly) to the phatic function of language. He describes (150) the phatic function as the dominant function in 'conversation' (by which he appears to mean casual, spontaneous conversation, or what I have called 'chats', where the interactional level takes precedence over any accompanying transactional level). Leech does not, however, expand his remarks to any detailed discussion of the various forms which phatic communion might take throughout this kind of encounter.

As my earlier summary of Malinowski's work shows, the original definition of phatic communion clearly covers more than simply 'ice-breaking' and 'silence-filling' functions of language and, as I shall show in subsequent chapters, it is not always dull, pedestrian and inoffensive.

One writer who does take a rather more 'extended' view of phatic communion is Turner (1973), who defines phatic language as that which is: 'designed more to accommodate and acknowledge a hearer than to carry a message' (212) (which accords with my distinction between interactional and transactional language).

Turner points out that we can include in phatic communion not only the language used in greetings and partings, but also 'friendly linguistic devices for achieving social camaraderie' (212).

He explains that phatic language recurs throughout any stretch of speech in the form of 'fillers' (ibid.), a term also used by Brown (1977: 107). These fillers are, however, only short phrases, such as *you know*, and extending the field of phatic communion to cover such as these does not bring Turner's view into line with that of Malinowski in 1923. There is, however, a further brief comment by Turner in the same work which indicates his acknowledgement of longer and more interactionally meaningful stretches of phatic communion. Although, in general (in common with most writers who discuss phatic communion) his comments focus on the use of phatic communion to signal friendliness, politeness and so on, he does mention (210) that:

There is a negative counterpart of the friendly phatic intention of language in jeering and sneering, where the intention is this time less to convey information than to exclude. Among children this intention may be manifested in special intonation. Occasionally among good friends abusive language is used with friendly intention. A rather more complex intention, where a desire both to wound and to caress compete, may lead to teasing.

There is some slight ambiguity here, in that it is not quite clear whether Turner regards the 'the phatic intention' as being, by definition, 'friendly', or whether he regards the 'friendly phatic intention' as simply one aspect of the phatic intention, but the quote does reveal that Turner has some appreciation of the way different types of phatic communion can be used to signal different things at an interactional level.

This reference to the more aggressive aspect of phatic communion is unique in the recent literature, and is, in fact, closely linked to Malinowski's 1923 article, in which, in his discussion of the creation of 'bonds of personal union between people' (1923: 316) he notes that that there is a sub-category which he terms 'the bonds of antipathy'.

Turner's comments can be seen as closely following and, to some extent, providing a development of Malinowski's original observations, but Turner does not follow through with further argument and exemplification in this area.

The most detailed work on phatic communion is to be found in an article by Laver (1975), who deals first with the 'meaningless' aspect, and points out that the 'surface meaning' of the words used in phatic communion is by no means irrelevant: 'I would wish to take the position that the semantic meaning of the tokens selected in phatic communion is relevant to the nature of the interaction' (222) because, as he explains and exemplifies, the choice of the first phatic tokens in an opening phase constrains 'the semantic theme within which the participants must make their choices of tokens in a particular occasion of phatic communion'.

The main thrust of Laver's article is, however, an analysis of the function of phatic communion apart from its undoubted 'ice-breaking' function.

He divides 'interactions' (which are, in Laver's terminology, equivalent to what I have called 'encounters') into three parts—opening, medial and closing and claims that the 'main business' of an encounter is that which is carried out in the medial phase, the opening and closing phases serving to provide a framework for this 'main business'.

His comments and observations cover not only the language used in encounters, but also gestural and kinesic features, all of which he subsumes under the heading of phatic communion. As this work is concerned only with the LINGUISTIC give and take of encounters, I will refer only to those sections of Laver's argument which deal with what he refers to as the 'linguistic tokens' used in phatic communion.

He claims that the choice of a particular type of phatic opening or closing remark establishes or consolidates the particular type of relationship (in terms of status and/or solidarity) which is to hold between the speakers for the duration of the encounter. It will, perhaps, be helpful to give a brief outline here of the basic points of Laver's model.

1.4.1 Opening phases

Laver explains that speakers use the opening phase—which he defines as the beginning of the conversational encounter AFTER the exchange of formulaic greetings—to signal and establish an interpersonal framework for the encounter. They do this by their choice of self-oriented, other-oriented, or neutral opening utterances, and these choices are based on the relative status of the participants in the following ways:

1. Where an admitted inferior opens an encounter with an admitted superior (the participants being in a non-solidary relationship), the inferior will open with a self-oriented remark, such as *hot work this*, thus acknowledging the right of the superior to invade the psychological world of the inferior, and, by this remark, inviting him to do so. The inferior participant is not allowed to invade the psychological world of the superior, as this would infringe the status rules which hold between them.

2. Where the admitted superior opens an encounter such as the one described in (1) above, he will use an other-oriented remark, such as *that looks like hot work*, again signalling his right and duty to invade the psychological world of the inferior. He will not use a self-oriented remark, as both parties know that the inferior speaker is not allowed into the psychological world of the superior, and a self-oriented opener by the superior would, therefore, only emphasise the status barrier between them, by not allowing the inferior to respond.

3. Where two social equals begin an encounter, they are most likely to use a neutral opener, such as a comment about the weather. This neutral category is also often used to open encounters between non-equals, as it avoids the problem of choosing either a self- or other-oriented token, where, perhaps, the relative status of the participants is not clear.

4. Where the encounter is between participants who do share a solidary relationship, whatever their relative social status, there is a free choice of opener, as the solidarity between them takes precedence over their relative status.

1.4.2 Closing phases

Laver claims that closing phases of encounters function and operate in a similar way to opening phases, but that, instead of setting up the interpersonal framework for the bulk of the encounter, they function to sum up what the interpersonal relationship has been, and very often make references to possible future meetings, thus helping to present the current encounter as part of a chain of meetings. During the progression of the speakers towards actual cessation of talk and parting there is, according to Laver, a strong likelihood that the participant who initiates the closing will make reference to some factor outside the encounter, which is presented as a REASON for closing. Good reasons are needed so as to 'mitigate the potential sense of rejection that a participant might feel when his fellow participant initiates the closing phase' (1975: 230)

Neutral tokens are rarely used in closings—Laver claims that the over-whelming tendency is for speakers to use either 'self' or 'other' oriented tokens (apart from what he describes as the 'formulaic forms of farewell').

1.4.3 Phatic communion as interactional language

Laver's article does, then, make a substantial contribution to the under-standing of phatic communion, as it provides a detailed model of how such utterances function in dialogue. It is strange, however, that, like other writers (and unlike Malinowski), he restricts the OCCASIONS of phatic communion to opening and closing phases of encounters—it is, for him, essentially an 'ice-breaking' function of language, very similar to the 'access rituals' described by Goffman (1971: 79) which occur at the boundaries of 'heightened social access'; those linguistic exchanges, in other words, which allow speakers to move from non-encounter to encounter and out again.

My own interpretation of phatic communion (although influenced to some extent by the observations made by the writers referred to in the preceding paragraphs) is based on Malinowski's original definition and description. It is most clearly viewed as contrasting with Speech-in-action, in that it is a kind of language which is unrelated to any action which the speakers may be performing at the time of talk. Where phatic communion is in progress, the situation, for the speakers, IS the exchanging of phatic communion. Its purpose, then, is not to further any action currently in progress, nor to cause or further any action in the world in the future—it is to enable the speakers to relate to one another through the use of language, without consideration of the needs of the 'outside' world.

This means that phatic communion can, as other writers point out, occur as short words or phrases among other, non-phatic speech, and it can also (and often does) extend over a whole encounter (such as a chat), which may last for several hours.

Phatic language is, in fact, the same phenomenon as that which I have referred to as 'interactional language'. I shall, however, retain the term 'interaction(al)' (and 'interactive') throughout this work, because, as the preceding paragraphs show, there has been, since 1923, a strong tendency for linguists to understate the extent to which phatic communion dominates dialogue, and to view it as occurring ONLY in short phrases amidst other, more 'important' uses of language. So pronounced is this tendency, that I consider it best to retain an alternative term, so as not to cause any confusion.

2 Goal and status

2.1 Goal

I have, in the Introduction to this work, introduced the notion of different kinds of goal in conversation, and made a distinction between TRANSACTIONAL and INTERACTIONAL goals. This distinction, although useful in many ways, should not be taken to imply that any given utterance MUST be either interactional or transactional—there may often be components of both in the same utterance. Similarly, with whole encounters, both kinds of goal may be in operation, although, in most encounters, it is possible to observe which is the dominant goal.

In an encounter between, for example, buyer and seller in a shop, there may well be (and usually is) some form of interactive goal observable in the speech behaviour of the participants; e.g. expressions of politeness may be exchanged, along with matching evaluations of the weather, etc. The interactive level in such an encounter is, however, clearly subordinate to the transactional goal of selling/buying goods of some kind. The reverse of this may occur within a primarily interactional encounter, such as a casual chat with a friend, during which some kind of transaction may well take place (accompanied by transactional speech), such as the borrowing of bus fare. Again, although the encounter exhibits characteristics of both interactional and transactional speech, reflecting the two types of goal, it is clear that the interactional level is dominant.

As these comments imply, I am, in discussing conversational 'goal', concentrating on OVERALL goal—the general purpose of the conversation—rather than the moment-by-moment goals which may, and do, arise during the discourse. Schank's 1977 paper on 'Rules and Topics in Conversation' refers to 'local and global topics', in order to distinguish between short-term, 'temporary' topics, and long-term, 'what the conversation is really about' topics; my concern with conversational goals can be said to be in the area of 'global' rather than 'local' goals, although I shall, of course, in subsequent chapters, make some reference to local conversational goals, particularly when they can be seen to be operating to further some global goal.

2.2 Status

As section 0.3 of the Introduction to this work indicates, an important component of conversation is the relative status of the participants. The acknowledgement and expression of relative status has two functions in dialogue:

1. it in part defines the TYPE of conversational encounter, and
2. it enables speakers to pursue the GOAL of the encounter.

These two functions of status can, in a sense, be compared to the two types of goal-differentiated verbal encounter, transactional and interactional, in that the first function is primarily concerned with the organisation of the speech encounter as an event in the 'outside' world which is made up of a series of events, while the second function is primarily concerned with the structure and organisation of the inner workings of the discourse. This requires some further discussion and explanation:

If we first consider ways of defining the type of speech encounter, we can see that status functions in this area to link the talk of the encounter with the cultural events and institutions of the society within which the encounter occurs. That is, the status of speakers in the outside world, or what can be referred to as their 'official' status (e.g. 'managing director', 'employer', 'secretary', 'tutor', 'student', 'doctor', 'patient'), is crucial to the definition of certain speech encounters, which actually DEPEND upon that official status. For an encounter to be recognised as a tutorial, for instance (or, more accurately, for an encounter to BE a tutorial), it must involve an exchange of talk between at least one tutor and at least one student. Furthermore, it is not sufficient for the meeting to be between two people who just 'happen' to be employed as a tutor and a student—two such people may meet and talk for a variety of different reasons; if their meeting is to be a tutorial, they must each carry their official status into the meeting and use it overtly in the management of the discourse, so that one speaker is BEING the tutor, and the other is BEING the student.

Similarly, if the encounter is to be a chat, then the speakers must relinquish their official status, and any status differential which exists between them in the outside world. A speaker may not 'be' a tutor during a chat without the encounter changing its nature and becoming a tutorial, because 'being' a tutor involves the speaker adopting a superior orientation towards the hearer, who is thereby pressurised to adopt the role of inferior, by 'being' the student.

It is, of course, clear that this arrangement of status patterning as superior/inferior, or equal/equal, is very much a game for two players (AT LEAST two players, that is) in that the notion of 'superior' is only possible if there is an 'inferior', and, in the same way, speakers can only be 'equal' in status if they agree to be so.

Now to consider what I have referred to as the second function of status in dialogue (enabling the speakers to pursue their conversational goal). As the preceding paragraphs explain, the introduction of official status into an encounter such as a chat redefines the nature of that encounter. In a similar way, the adoption of equal/equal status patterning in an encounter such as a tutorial, which is characterised by a superior/inferior status patterning, will transform the tutorial into a chat (or a row, a fight, etc.). This, of course, means that the overall goal of the encounter is changed—what speakers 'aim for' in a tutorial is not what they aim for in a chat; a tutorial has, in fact, a transactional goal, whereas a chat has an interactional goal. So the goal of an encounter is intimately tied to the status patterns created by the speakers; if the 'normal' status pattern for a particular encounter (or type of encounter) is preserved, then this enables the speakers to pursue their overall goal—if that 'normal' status pattern is changed, then speakers are unable to pursue their original goal.

I have said that relative status has two major functions in dialogue—it must also be remembered that any individual speaker can, under different circumstances, be classified in different ways according to his/her own status, and the various types of status which can be assigned to a speaker mesh with these two major functions.

It can be said that, in any dialogue, the status of a speaker can be classified, broadly speaking, in two ways:

1. Status external to the encounter, i.e. social or socio-economic status in the world; this is generally a fixed, or at least long-term personal feature of a speaker.
2. Status internal to the encounter, i.e. that adopted by or assigned to a speech participant in a particular encounter (or part of an encounter) with regard to a particular topic under discussion, *vis-à-vis* his/her co-conversationalist; this is, of course, a very temporary personal feature, typically varying throughout a particular encounter, depending on the varying roles adopted by the speaker through a progression of topics.

2.3 Fixed status and transactional encounters

The 'fixed' nature of external status has an important bearing on the ROLES a speaker may adopt in an encounter. Some particular cases of external status may be so fixed that they are, in a wide variety of speech events, inescapable; this is the case with certain individuals whose external status is such that it amounts to a special kind of fame, for example, members of the royal family. Such individuals are constrained by their external status to play only a very narrow range of roles in most encounters other than those which take place within their immediate circle of intimates.

This is not, of course, the case with most speakers, but there are, nevertheless, many speech events which involve ordinary citizens in acting out only those roles which are appropriate to their external status. Such speech events are those in which what Mathiot and Dougherty (1978: 214) refer to as the 'event structure' predominates. The event structure is the set of speaker roles which relates to the expected, predictable progress of events, and Mathiot and Dougherty contrast this with 'role structure', which relates to the unpredictable orientation of participants towards those events. The event structure is, then, the set of roles which furthers the transactional goal, and role structure is the set which furthers the interactional goal.

Speech encounters which are dominated by external status are, in fact, those in which the TRANSACTIONAL goal is paramount, and in which any interactional goal is subordinate (though often instrumental) to this.

Such encounters are frequently associated with some kind of cultural institution, so that the participants can be seen as enacting institutional roles; that is, they are acting, not as individual human beings, but as 'types', and the particular roles they adopt in any given encounter are complementary 'pair types', involving either a superior, and an inferior participant—for example, teacher/pupil, employer/employee, doctor/patient—or two equal participants—for example, a meeting between two heads of state.

Throughout such encounters, speakers may well make minor adjustments in their relative status, but will (even in interactional phases during the transaction) keep within their appointed, complementary roles preserving the status balance between them.

This preservation of fixed status is essential if the nature of the encounter is to be kept constant; a 'lesson' is only a lesson if one participant is 'being the teacher' throughout and at least one other participant is 'being the pupil', and a doctor/patient consultation is only that if someone is 'being the doctor' and someone else is 'being the patient'. Participants may not (even if they continue to discuss a topic directly related to the transactional goal of the encounter) exchange roles—just as the status balance is 'fixed', so are the actors-out of the appropriate roles. In encounters such as this, a change of status means a change of encounter type in the same way as does a change of goal.

A transactional encounter, being based on fixed, external status, is, then, in a sense, a rigid framework for communication, characterised by restrictions in the areas of status patterning, overall transactional goal, and (resulting from the goal restrictions) topic range. In an encounter between non-equals, responsibility for managing the progress of the encounter lies, of course, with the superior participant. Chapter 3 will illustrate the ways in which this management is carried out, by reference to examples from job interviews and a tutorial. The aspects discussed will be: initial and final interaction, overt signalling of status, and topic introduction and management.

2.4 Variable status and interactional encounters

Encounters which are dominated by the 'role structure' rather than the 'event structure' allow participants to form varying status patterns throughout the dialogue; unlike fixed status encounters, participants are not constrained to adopt only those roles which will produce status patterns appropriate to a particular transactional goal.

This freedom from constraints should not, however, be taken to mean that, within a variable status encounter (which can, of course, be equated with an interactional encounter), ANY roles are open to the participants. There are many roles which are disallowed in such encounters, precisely those roles, in fact, which are appropriate to fixed status encounters, and which are adopted in pursuance of transactional goals. The adoption of a role which reflects fixed status will, in an interactional encounter, have one of two possible effects. The nature of the encounter may be automatically changed, e.g. when a married couple who work together as non-equals move from a chat into a work-directed transaction; or the adoption of the inappropriate fixed status role may be overtly labelled as inappropriate by the 'hearer', e.g. when a teacher returns home from work still in 'teaching mode' and is told by his/her spouse 'keep your classroom manner for the classroom'.

Co-conversationalists in an interactional encounter are, then (as are those in a transactional encounter), constrained to use only the set of roles (and consequent status patterns) which are appropriate to the speech event.

In spite of this constraint, interactional speech participants do have a degree of freedom in their adoption of status which is not possible for transactional speech participants. This 'freedom' (of which one aspect is, in fact, 'obligation') lies in the EXCHANGEABILITY of roles in interactional encounters, and the resultant reversal of status patterns, in terms of superior/inferior. In other words, speakers in variable status, interactional encounters, TAKE TURNS at being superior and inferior. This means that they are, in fact, in a basic interactional state of being 'equal', in that they have equal rights (and duties) to take on various roles throughout the encounter, though this equality may exist only within the encounter because in terms of external status they may well be non-equals.

The balance of this equality is, because of the constantly varying status patterns, a matter for close collaboration and monitoring throughout interactional encounters, and, as Chapter 5 will illustrate, there are occasions when the balance is destroyed by a speaker who forgets, or ignores, the basic rule of exchanging roles, and when extensive work has to be done on topic management in order to restore an acceptable interactional balance to the encounter.

Chapter 3 will deal in some detail with the workings of transactional encounters, paying particular attention to formal job interviews, and Chapter 4 will describe the interactional basis of variable status encounters.

3 Transactional (fixed status) encounters

This chapter will deal with the way status functions in the management of primarily transactional encounters; the data used for the discussion will be drawn from two kinds of fixed status encounters:

1. Job interviews where the participants are previously unknown to one another. These will provide examples of encounters where the transactional goal takes precedence over all other aspects of the dialogue.
2. Tutorials where the participants are well known to one another. This is not such a clear-cut case (in the area of goal definition) as the job interviews; there is, of course, in a tutorial, a transactional goal—in the tutorial which provides the examples for this section, the transactional goal is to discuss and evaluate a student essay, and to provide guidance for the student in forthcoming examinations. A tutorial is also, however, an encounter which is likely to have a large interactional component—being largely a matter of the tutor reassuring the student. This interactional component is, however, a way of pursuing the overall transactional goal of improving the student's academic performance. In a tutorial, then, we would expect to find interactional phases occurring throughout the encounter.

3.1 An analysis of job interviews

3.1.1 Opening phases in job interviews

A job interview is clearly an example of a fixed status encounter, with a primarily transactional goal, where the superior participant (the interviewer) takes his status 'in the world' INSIDE the encounter—he is the superior participant in the particular encounter BECAUSE OF his status in the world, and, because the encounter is a job interview, it is his status with regard to his paid occupation or official position which is relevant.

A job interview is, then, what Laver would describe as an encounter between an ACKNOWLEDGED superior and an ACKNOWLEDGED inferior in a non-solidary relationship. According to Laver, the rules for opening such an encounter are slightly different, depending on which participant does the opening, but, in a case such as a job interview, this consideration does not really apply, as the encounter opens at a specific, mutually agreed time, fixed in advance—it is not opened by the unilateral decision of one participant. Following Laver as far as possible, however, we can expect to find that, whichever participant makes the opening remark, the tokens used will be oriented towards the psychological world of the inferior, the interviewee. It is unlikely that a neutral opening token will be used as, again according to Laver, these tend to occur in encounters where the relative status of the participants, though unequal, may not be relevant to that encounter. The following examples will examine the data to discover whether job interviews do, in fact, open with what I term an 'interactional phase', which sets up (or reinforces) the interpersonal framework for the 'main business' of the encounter, and whether, if this is the case, the tokens used in these interactional opening phases are, indeed, oriented towards the psychological world of the inferior participant.

Example (1) Tape—Keyte.

Interviewer: this is Mrs Cheepen . let me introduce you to these (inaud.) this is Mrs Scott . the ə personnel assistant

Interviewee: *how do you do*

Scott: *how do you do* . pleased to meet you

Keyte: +how do you do+

Interviewee: +how do you do+

Interviewer: +(inaud.)+ principal personnel officer and Mr Dudley who is senior *admin officer*

Dudley: *hello* . +how do you do+

Interviewee: +how do you do+

Interviewer: please have a seat Mrs Cheepen

Interviewee: thank you -------

Keyte: did you have a good trip

Interviewee: yes very nice . beautiful day . *lovely bus journey*

Interviewer: *(inaud.)*

Keyte: oh you came on the bus +did you+

Interviewer: +yes+

Keyte: oh -- əm - so have you been to County Hall before

Interviewee: a long time ago .

Keyte: *mm*

Interviewee: *very long* time ago it's years since I've been out here

Keyte: +mhm+

Interviewee: +it's very+ nice this time of year with all the trees
Keyte: yes . yes . well we we like it here
Scott: *(laugh)*
Interviewee: *yes . (inaud.)* --
Keyte: you've been in the offices . years ago . yes
Interviewee: not in the offices .
Keyte: no . +no+
Interviewee: +at County Hall+
Keyte: no (inaud.) - right well ə. əm . ə the the panel here have got various things to əask you (etc.)

The formal introductory phase with which this extract opens, and which precedes what can be seen as the interactional opening remarks apparently envisaged by Laver, involves the use of references to official status. The use of such references here not only functions to establish the status differential which provides the interpersonal framework for the encounter—it is, of course, as the encounter is a JOB interview, also transactionally relevant, because it gives the interviewee some information about the hierarchy within the institution where the job vacancy has occurred.

After the formal introduction, there is, in this extract, clearly an interactional phase (which appears, in this rather formal setting, to be composed largely of formulaic tokens of politeness) and, as Laver suggests, the opening remarks are, indeed, oriented towards the psychological world of the inferior participant:

did you have a good trip (etc.)

This patterning does, of course, reinforce the status differential of which all the participants are already aware, but, whereas Laver implies that this is the sole function of such an opening phase, there is evidence, in this particular encounter, that there is an additional function.

Towards the end of the encounter, the subject matter of this opening phase is reinvoked by the interviewer, and shown to be relevant to the overall TRANSACTIONAL goal of the interview:

Example (2) Tape—Keyte
Keyte: how about əm actually getting from St. Albans to County Hall on a regular basis is there is there a good bus service *you came on the bus*
Interviewee: *yes*
Keyte: today (etc.)

As this later extract shows, the interviewer (Keyte) has used the information gained in the opening, apparently purely interactional, phase as a piece of transactional information. It is as though this opening topic has, in some way, been 'saved up' until it could be reinvoked as relevant to the transaction. This operation seems to have similarities with certain of the 'closing devices' described by Schegloff and Sacks (1974). A typical device in such a situation is, according to Schegloff and Sacks, a reference BACK to a topic already covered earlier in the conversation: 'Such materials can be picked up any place in a conversation and seemingly be preserved for use in the conversation's closing' (1974: 250), and, as they point out, these reinvoked topics frequently originate at the opening of conversation, and are concerned with activities in which the receiver of the call was involved, and which were interrupted by the opening of the conversation. The example of this device in the Keyte tape is very similar to the kind of example referred to by Schegloff and Sacks, although it is not, in this case, closing-oriented, and serves to illustrate that the general notion of 'preserving' topics for use later on is a valid one.

Example (3) Tape—Gilbey
Interviewee: *hallo*
Gilbey: *hallo* --- do have a seat
Interviewee: thank you very much ---
Gilbey: well thank you very much indeed for coming today . *very pleased to see you*
Interviewee: *(inaud.)*
Gilbey: perhaps I ought to start by introducing us all . əm my name's Mr Gilbey I'm Assistant County Personnel Officer
Interviewee: mhm
Gilbey: this is Mr . Tibbles who's a . personnel officer and this is Rob Woodhull who's the administrative officer who would be your immediate
Interviewee: ah yes
Gilbey: superior . əif you were to get the job . did you have any trouble getting here today
Interviewee: no (inaud.)
Gilbey: car parking OK
Interviewee: well I came on the bus today actually
Gilbey: *did you*
Interviewee: *and the* bus was on time +yes+
Gilbey: +that's+ a bit of a walk up is it it it's raining out there *did you*
Interviewee: *oh no*
Gilbey: manage to keep dry
Interviewee: it's not it's not far from the bus stop actually
Gilbey: fine . right --- now . just to start by əasking you (etc.)

As in the Keyte tape, there is clearly some kind of interactional phase after what Laver refers to as 'formulaic greetings', and before the 'main business' of the interview begins, involving such utterances as:

> thank you very much indeed for coming today .
> very pleased to see you

which, again, appears to be classifiable as an other-oriented token which invades the psychological world of the inferior participant, and the extract proceeds in very much the same way as the Keyte tape.

Again, this extract shows (as in the Keyte tape) how a superior participant can make overt reference to the status differential within which the interview takes place, by means of references to official status:

Example (4) Tape—Gilbey

Gilbey: perhaps I ought to start by introducing us all . əm my name's Mr Gilbey I'm Assistant County Personnel Officer

Interviewee: mhm

Gilbey: this is Mr . Tibbles who's a . personnel officer and this is Rob Woodhull who's the administrative officer who would be your immediate

Interviewee: ah yes

Gilbey: superior . əif you were to get the job .

As in the Keyte tape, all the members of the interview board are referred to by name, in combination with explicit reference to their job descriptions. However, in this example, it is interesting to note that Gilbey makes further status distinctions between the members of the board. To those members of the board who hold senior positions (himself and Tibbles) he assigns the address form Title plus Last Name, whereas to the junior member he assigns First Name plus Last Name.

In this interview, then, the status differential is underlined, in the opening, interactional phase, not only by the rather subtle tactic of inferior-oriented remarks—it is also overtly stated by the differentiation in address terms used by Gilbey, the Chairman of the interview board.

The setting up of an unambiguous interpersonal framework for the encounter is not always, then, exclusively a delicate operation of manipulating 'self'- or 'other'-oriented tokens throughout the opening, interactional phase—it can, as in this and the Keyte tape, be brought fully into focus and be made verbally explicit.

Those academic interviews transcribed in the London–Lund Corpus volume which contain opening phases differ from the job interviews extracts which are given in Examples 1–4 above, in that, although there clearly are initial phases of interaction, they tend to be very short, and although oriented by the superior participant towards the inferior participant (thereby following Laver's 'rule' of the superior invading the psychological world of the inferior), they are so formulaic (e.g. *how are you*)—tokens which, in Laver's model fall, in fact, OUTSIDE the 'opening', interactional phase—as almost to render this 'invasion' null and void. They fall, in fact, into the category of ordinary, unremarkable politeness (see Texts 3.1a and 3.1c, LLC).

Before leaving this section of the discussion, there is one further point which should be made with regard to the Gilbey tape. Immediately after the introduction of the members of the interview board (with reference to their status), there follows:

Example (5) Tape—Gilbey.
Gilbey: did you have any trouble getting here today
Interviewee: no (inaud.)
Gilbey: car parking OK
Interviewee: well I came on the bus today actually (etc., and later in the interview):
Gilbey: and travel as well how does that əfit in with your . plans
Interviewee: oh well there's there's no problem about that cause it's not really that far . from St. Albans it's quite easy
Gilbey: it's about half an hour I *expect*
Interviewee: *yes* yes
Tibbles: so . have you got one car (etc.)

As the extracts show, the same topic is discussed here as in the Keyte tape—the mode of transport used by the interviewee—and again, the superior participant in this encounter has, at the second mention (during the main part of the interview), reinvoked the topic transactionally. The fact that both the interview tapes show the introduction of this topic AND its reinvocation later in the conversation appears to indicate that this is typical of job interviews; it seems to be a topic which should be MENTIONED early on in the encounter, but discussed in more detail at a later time, after topics such as past work experience, educational achievements, etc.

N.B. My own corpus contains yet another example of this reinvocation of mode of travel as a topic for discussion—this time in an interactional conversation (CELIA); for details of this, see Chapter 5, p. 101.

3.1.2 Interactional breaks during transaction

In highly formalised, fixed status encounters, such as job interviews, it is rare to find interactional phases during the medial, transactional phase, but the Gilbey tape does, in fact, contain examples of this. The circumstances are, however, extraordinary; while the interview is in progress, building work is being carried out on the floor above, and there are occasional noises of crashing masonry, which are loud enough actually to disrupt the interview. The participants, unable to ignore the noises, introduce them as an interactional topic of conversation:

Example (6) Tape—Gilbey
Gilbey: have to excuse the rats (laugh) *(inaud.)*
Interviewee: *(inaud., laugh)*
Tibbles: we can all relax together in this
All: (laugh)
Gilbey: yes this this seems to be the you know . trouble with the rodents
                in the roof anyway *(inaud.)*
Interviewee: *(inaud.)*
Gilbey: we'll try and ignore it
Interviewee: (laugh)
Gilbey: and sorry for that

As the extract shows, one of the participants (Tibbles) makes an overt reference to the fact that the conversation has become, at least temporarily, interactional:

WE CAN ALL RELAX TOGETHER IN THIS.

Later in the interview, there are two similar disruptions, and, on each occasion, the participants enter a short phase of interaction:

Example (7) Tape—Gilbey
Woodhull: (....)the section for which I am responsible --
(LOUD NOISE)
                INTERACTION
                əm sorry . it isn't true that the last person who had the job we've
                stuck up in the roof *and*
Interviewee: *(laugh)*
                RETURN TO TRANSACTION
Woodhull: they're . əwe we actually if you like provide support to
                everybody else and it's our . it's our job to deal (etc.)

and:

Example (8) Tape—Gilbey
Woodhull: I think that's a fair description of what we try and do ---
(LOUD NOISE)
                INTERACTION
Tibbles: I think it's always also worth . ensuring you that THE JOB IS NOT
                IN THIS BUILDING
Interviewee: (laugh) *oh thank God for that*
Gilbey: *(inaud.)*
Interviewee: (laugh)
                RETURN TO TRANSACTION
Tibbles: IT'S OVER AT CENTRAL OFFICE

On this last occasion, however, Tibbles uses his interactional comment on it in order to impart TRANSACTIONAL information—i.e. letting the interviewee know where the job is (somewhere other than the site of the interview)—and he thus returns the conversation to the pursuit of the transactional goal of suiting job vacancy to job applicant. This kind of medial interaction is, of course, rare in job interviews, and occurs here only because of extraordinary factors in the environment which threaten to disrupt the transaction.

3.1.3 Closing phases in job interviews

If Laver's comments on closing phases are correct, we would expect to find that the closing phases of job interviews reflect the status differential which has been the interpersonal framework throughout the interview, and, according to Laver, this is likely to be expressed, not by neutral tokens, but by either 'self'- or 'other-oriented' tokens.

The nature of the status differential which exists in job interviews dictates that this would mean the delivery of 'other-oriented' tokens by the superior participant, thus reinforcing his/her superiority over the inferior participant (the interviewee). Extracts from the transcriptions will show, however, that, although the status differential is, indeed, reinforced, this is not achieved in the way Laver suggests.

Example (9) Tape—Gilbey
Woodhull: no . no more questions
Gilbey: well I'd like to thank you very much for coming today *əm*
Interviewee: *(inaud.)*
Gilbey: əm obviously we've a number of candidates to see
Interviewee: +mhm+
Gilbey: +so+ əm we can't . make let you know straight away
Interviewee: mm
Gilbey: we would hope to make a decision very quickly and be in touch
             with you within the week
Interviewee: *OK that's fine*
Gilbey: *so . əif you'd like to find your way out I'm sure you can +find
             your way+
Interviewee: +(inaud.)+
Gilbey: through the maze of corridors
Woodhull: *nice to meet you*
Interviewee: *thank you very much* bye bye
Gilbey: bye bye
Woodhull: cheerio

Example (10) Tape—Keyte
Keyte: well I think that's fine *thank you very much*

Interviewee: *OK* +thank you very much (inaud.)+
Keyte: +and we'll write to you+ within the next two or three days
Interviewee: thank you very much *nice to have met you*
Keyte: *thank you for coming*
Scott: +bye+
Interviewer: +bye+

Both these extracts include a reference to contact in the future (by letter), but this is not, of course, an interactional reference—the letters referred to are concerned with the possible offer of a job, and the references are, therefore, very much part of the transactional aspect of the encounter; it would, in fact, be strange to find an example of interactional reference to future contact in a job interview between people who have never met before.

There is, in both extracts, a phenomenon noted by Laver in the majority of closing phases—a comment about the quality of the current encounter—*nice to meet you* from the superior participant in the Gilbey tape, and *nice to have met you* from the inferior in the Keyte tape.

Apart from this, however, the extracts do not fall into line with the model described by Laver, in that there are no interactional remarks which reinforce the interpersonal framework of the encounter. The speakers use only formulaic tokens of farewell, and politeness rituals such as *thank you*.

The academic interviews in the London–Lund Corpus publication show a similar pattern, and it seems from this that Laver's explanation of the status reinforcing function of the closing phase of encounters is incorrect, at least in the case of interviews between strangers.

On further consideration, however, it becomes evident that these rather 'bare' closing phases do, in fact, reflect and reinforce the interpersonal status balance which has characterised the encounter, though not in the way that Laver describes. Interviews are, as I have pointed out, 'fixed status encounters'—there is a predetermined status differential between the interviewer(s), who is the superior participant, and the interviewee, who is the inferior participant. This fixed, unequal status means that all aspects of the encounter are within the control of the interviewer, and this, of course, includes the termination of the interview. Both participants know that it is the right and the duty of the interviewer to initiate closing, so there is no 'sense of rejection' on the part of the interviewee, and, therefore, no need for mitigating interactional devices. The paucity of interactional tokens in closing phases of interviews is, then, the reflection and reinforcement of the interpersonal framework of the encounter.

3.1.4 Topic control

In primarily interactional encounters, topic control is very much a matter of negotiation between speakers; it is often a complex process, involving subtle manoeuvring, which will be discussed in detail in Chapter 4. In job interviews, however, which are primarily transactional, and governed by fixed status, it is a comparatively simple phenomenon.

Generally speaking, all rights and duties connected with topic control are the province of the interviewer, and there is a particular phenomenon associated with topic control by the superior participant in an interview, which is, of course, rarely found in primarily interactional dialogue, though typical of classroom discourse (as described by Sinclair and Coulthard 1975)—this is the METASTATEMENT:

Example (11) Tape—Keyte
Keyte: the the panel here have got various things to əask you obviously about this job . and əm - Mrs. ə. Scott here will . əm take . you know . descr əm . y talk to you about the . a . the job . itself

Example (12) Tape—Keyte
Scott: what I wanted to do was just sort of . go through it

Example (13) Tape—Keyte
Keyte: well we've discussed the job perhaps we ought now to look . in . əm . at your . educational achievements
Interviewee: *mhm*
Keyte: *and then possibly discuss after that your əm . previous experience
Interviewee: yes
Keyte: as relating to this job and then we can
Interviewer: can I ask you *(inaud.)*
Keyte: *ask you some questions (inaud.)*
Interviewer: background educational background

This repeated use of the metastatement displays the invariable superior status of the interviewer in the encounter, and also illustrates the similarity between this kind of dialogue and that which takes place between teacher and pupils in the classroom.

Another phenomenon, somewhat similar to the metastatement, tends to characterise unequal encounters (of which a job interview is one particular manifestation), that is, what Thomas (1985: 767) refers to as a 'metapragmatic act'. One kind of metapragmatic act which is, according to Thomas's data, frequently performed by the superior speaker in unequal discourse, is a 'Restrospective comment' (771), which operates to indicate unambiguously the exact illocutionary intent of the speaker. There is an example of one such in my corpus:

Example (14) Tape—Keyte
Scott: I just wanted to you know you will not be meeting the public face to face I just wanted to make that clear to you

This is, however, the only example of a retrospective comment in my corpus, but this is not really surprising, because the unequal encounters I am dealing with are job interviews (and one, very amicable, tutorial). The data on which Thomas's comments are based consist of unequal encounters where the power of the superior speaker is used overtly AGAINST the inferior speaker (her examples are drawn from disciplinary interviews in which the inferior speaker is clearly 'on the carpet'). This is not, of course, the case with job interviews, although it is interesting to note that the academic interviews (interviews for prospective students) transcribed in the London–Lund corpus contain far more overtly power-laden utterances than do the job interviews in my corpus.

In addition to metapragmatic acts, Thomas also describes and exemplifies 'upshots' and 'reformulations', both tactics used by the superior speaker in an unequal (heavily power-laden and, therefore, face-threatening) encounter, and occurrences of these are plentiful in the academic interviews of the London–Lund Corpus—an example of an upshot would be:

Example (15) London-Lund Corpus. Tape—S.3.1. (p. 762)
a: [ə:] have you read any Chaucer
A: yes - only - you know . the first . I've read Patient Griselda . that's not Chaucer I'm afraid . *[ə:m]*
B: *you* read The Clerk's you read The Clerk's Tale you mean --
A: [m] .[n] yes . but that was also pre - this is also rather in the mists of antiquity
a: in other words [ə:] you can't remember very much about it

and an example of a reformulation:

Example (16) London-Lund Corpus. Tape—S.3.5 (p. 861)
a: *can you . can you . exemplify (2 to 3 sylls.)*
A: [əm] well I *wouldn't think he'd disapprove of the Pardoner - I I suppose he does - [ə:] consciously -- but [ə] -- he he sees him [ə] -- rather mischievously . and [ə]
a: [ə:] it's rather more serious than that isn't it

There is a further similarity between classroom discourse and interviews, and examples of it abound in the Keyte and Gilbey tapes—this is the use of what Sinclair and Coulthard refer to as a 'marker' (realised by items such as 'right', 'well', followed by 'silent stress'), which is one of the 'acts' which compose a 'framing move' (1975: 44). Framing moves occur in classroom discourse at the boundaries between topics or sub-topics, and the same phenomenon can be observed in interviews:

Example (17) Tape—Gilbey
Interviewee: əm yes I've done a job similar to this before for St. Albans City
            Council so I'm familiar with most of that kind of thing
Gilbey: fine WELL . you have obviously əhad experience in local
            government but I . wonder if it might be helpful to you if I ask
            əRob to əm fill you in on what the County Secretary's
            Department does and how it fits in

These markers function in a similar way to the metastatements—to divide topics into clearly defined areas—and, like the metastatements, they are used, in interviews, by the superior participant in pursuance of his duty of managing topic progression.

The only occasions on which the interviewee has control of the topic are those on which she is specifically invited, by the interviewer, to take control:

Example (18) Tape—Gilbey
Gilbey: have you got the əm questions or queries you want to raise
            before we start

Example (19) Tape—Gilbey
Gilbey: fine well we've asked you a lot of questions əm . I wonder
            whether there's anything you'd like to ask us

There is also one occasion on which the interviewer appears to hand the control of topic to the interviewee, while actually specifying the narrow area from which the topic must be chosen:

Example (20) Tape—Keyte.
Keyte: have you got any queries about the conditions of service
            anything that you perhaps don't understand

Topic control is, then, throughout the interview, almost exclusively the responsibility of the interviewer.

3.1.5 Turn taking

In their detailed analysis of the ways in which 'turns at talk' are organised, Sacks, Schegloff and Jefferson (1978) describe what they term the 'turn allocational component'. The rules which govern this component cover all the possibilities of speaker change—i.e. selection of next speaker by current speaker, self-selection by next speaker, and, in the absence of these two possibilities, continuation of turn by current speaker until the next potential change-over point.

In primarily interactional dialogue, all these possibilities can, and do, become actualised, but in interviews the situation is rather different. The interview is not an 'ordinary' conversation—it is, rather, a highly formalised and predictable kind of encounter. Even though, in many interviews (including those used in this work), there may be more than one interviewer, it is rare to find dialogue taking place between members of the interview board; the talk is between the interviewee on one side and the members of the interview board on the other (who are, in fact, operating as one speaker). Members of the interview board plan which areas of the interview each individual will control in advance of the encounter, so there is no overlap between them, and no need for consultation during the encounter.

All parties to the interview have cultural knowledge of what an interview is, and of what is expected to happen during the interview—they know that the interviewer will introduce topics and ask questions, and that the interviewee will follow those topics and give appropriate answers. The allocation of conversational turns is built into the structure of the interview, and central to its nature, so the question of how next speakers are selected in interviews simply does not arise.

Length of conversational turn is, of course, determined in the same way as in all dialogue—possible take-over points being syntactic boundaries. It is, however, characteristic of interviews that, in the transactional phase, turns taken by the interviewee are, in general, longer than those which are typical of primarily interactional encounters because the purpose of an interview is to encourage and allow the interviewee to talk without interruption.

3.2 An analysis of a tutorial

3.2.1 Opening phase in tutorial

The tutorial which provides the data for this section is a fairly informal encounter, where the speech participants are well known to one another. This accounts for the informality of the opening phase when compared with the examples from the job interviews.

Example (21) Tape—Julie
(KNOCK ON DOOR)
Tutor: come in
Julie: hello
Tutor: hello ----
Tutor: have a seat - better this time
Julie: yeh . tired . I'm (inaud.) dead now I can't wake up . I'm think I'm
         thinking of going back to bed - ohh God
(TUTOR WALKS TO DOOR)

Tutor: first to ar first to arrive . that's ə. I wonder if there's anybody else ə. I
always get a *bit worried*
Julie: *somebody after me*
Tutor: yeh I know that there's there's somebody there's somebody all day
but I just wondered if the list was ə. the fact that the list is full means
that there are others . əwaiting in the . in the wings or if *that is all that
was interested*
Julie: *(inaud.)* --
Tutor: have you got your essay or have I got it . you *you've got it*
Julie: *I've got it*

Here, although the opening is informal (as though between equals), the status
differential is quite clearly established before the encounter even begins by the
fact that it is the tutee who presents herself at the office of the tutor and knocks
on the door to be admitted, even though the tutorial is by appointment and
she is expected to arrive at this time.

This kind of opening phase, which is very interactionally biased, in that it is
slanted very much towards the participants as individuals—note the self-
oriented tokens referring to inner states:

I'm ... dead now I can't wake up . I'm think I'm thinking of going back to bed
I wonder if ...
I always get a bit worried
I just wondered if...

tends not to occur in formal transactions, as the more formal the transaction,
the further the participants move from any attempt to create a shared world.

3.2.2 Closing phase in tutorial

Example (21) above shows that the opening phase of the encounter is likely
(particularly in an informal encounter where the participants are already well
acquainted) to have substantial interactional content. The closing phase is
similar:

Example (22) Tape—Julie
Tutor: reasonable to make sure you know what you're talking about first
Julie: yeh . right thank you
Tutor: right
Julie: see you later then
Tutor: see you əTuesday no Wednesday
Julie: (inaud.)
Tutor: (inaud.) I'll probably be around on Monday
Julie: (inaud.)
Tutor: watching you all doing phonetics

Julie: (inaud.)
Tutor: cheerio
Julie: see you

The interactional content in this closing phase is typical of the examples quoted by Laver, in that it contains 'explicit reference to the continuation of the relationship' (1975: 230) with:

> see you later
> see you Tuesday no Wednesday.

3.2.3 Interaction and topic movement

The influence of interaction in tutorials is not, however, restricted simply to Openings and Closings; there are occasions when the progress of the transaction is intimately linked to the ongoing interaction between the speakers, as in:

Example (23) Tape—Julie
(IMMEDIATELY AFTER OPENING INTERACTIONAL PHASE)
Tutor: were there any comments you had on the ə. on my comments
Julie: no not really ------
Tutor: (cough) yes it's totally different (etc.)

In this extract, the tutor invites Julie to comment, but she declines, and it appears, at this stage of the encounter, that she has nothing to say on the matter. Later in the tutorial, however (approximately eight minutes later), the tutor gives advice to Julie about how to tackle an imminent examination. He does this by using a series of imperatives:

> be positive pick the interpretation that suits you
> pick the interpretation that suits you best .
>   say that you're picking the interpretation
> say I interpret this to mean . əm . and then do it
> don't worry about it

thus expressing his superior status. At the end of this series of imperatives, the tutor brings his story to an end with:

Example (24) Tape—Julie
Tutor: ......so it's worth *having three areas*
Julie: *mm*
Tutor: generally . +planned+
Julie: +yeh+
Tutor: GONNA BE A HARD WEEK FOR YOU . phonetics and .

The emphasised part of the last utterance in this extract is clearly an interactional move, expressing sympathy with Julie by summing up what has already been discussed in the light of how it will affect her as an individual.

Julie then immediately begins a topic of her own choosing, but connected to what has gone before:

Example (25) Tape—Julie

Julie: I got my other piece of grammar back that were alright
Tutor: oh good . yeh there *you go*
Julie: *I got sixty for that*
Tutor: great
Julie: (inaud.)
Tutor: yeh
Julie: but I understand it more now anyway cause (inaud.) that much in there you know
Tutor: yeh
Julie: every day I think oh my God and I keep seeing it all these brackets in my head and
Tutor: yeh

Throughout this section of the encounter, as the above transcription shows, Julie continues with her topic, and the purpose of it is clearly interactional—she is telling the tutor about events in the past in order to tell him how she FEELS about her work now. He is responding on an interactional level by providing positive evaluations:

> oh good
> great,

which serve to encourage her to keep talking.

At the close of this interactional section the speakers move straight back to the 'main' business of the encounter, that is, they resume their pursuit of the transactional goal. Julie signals a topical break by the word *anyway*, and continues:

Example (26) Tape—Julie

Julie: OH I TELL YOU WHAT I WANTED TO ASK YOU I wrote some stuff down you know when e:m Bloomfield he əm . divides his əm word formation up and he has like primary . word . hang on can't remember now . primary word formation or something
Tutor: *mmhmm*
Julie: *and secondary*
Tutor: yeh
Julie: . well you know when he has əm primary and he has əm . that əm word formation with no free forms

Tutor: mmhmm
Julie: and then he has like receive . by inform by m by inform . well why
        does he ha why does he put ə then morpheme word like eat as a . a
        word without a free form . he has that in that group doesn't he
Tutor: ummm .
Julie: *he has*
Tutor: *no . * no I don't remember that . I didn't I don't remember he had it
        in that group
Julie: yes he has I've got it here
Tutor: mm
(ACADEMIC DISCUSSION FOLLOWS, FOR APPROXIMATELY
TWO MINUTES)
Julie: .....I've got that in notes I've made and I've got I'VE PUT THAT IN MY
        ESSAY . do you think I should check it (etc.)

As the emphasised sections at the beginning and end of this extract show,
Julie has held this as a possible topic for discussion throughout the tutorial
(which was, in fact, arranged in order to discuss the essay in question).

At the beginning of the encounter, however, in the extract already quoted
in Example (21) above, although she is explicitly invited by the tutor to raise
any points:

> were there any comments you had on the ə. on my comments
> no not really ------

she does not take up the invitation, even though the tutor does allow a long
pause to occur before taking the conversational floor himself. Instead, she
waits until much later in the encounter in order to raise the topic.

The reason for this is, I suggest, that the particular topic she wishes to raise
is one in which she has more background knowledge than the tutor. The topic
can, then, be seen as potentially troublesome at an interactional level, as it
overturns the status balance of the encounter (i.e. tutor = superior, student =
inferior), and it cannot, therefore, be introduced at just any point in the
encounter, even if she is invited to select the topic for discussion; it must,
somehow, be fitted onto the 'right' framework.

As Example (26) above shows, Julie has 'fitted' the introduction of this topic
to a preceding interactional phase, which has, itself, been initiated by the
tutor's interactional comment at the end of a previous transactional phase
(Example (22). The topic is raised, then, after a fairly prolonged phase of
interaction, which has been initiated by the superior participant. This phase
has, of course, involved (as do all interactions) a breaking down, to some
extent, of the status boundary which otherwise divides the speakers in an
unequal encounter, and the building up of some degree of interpersonal
solidarity in excess of that ordinarily afforded by the superior/inferior

framework. It is this temporary equality, which is established by a move to interactional, rather than directly transactional language, which allows Julie, who is throughout the encounter the inferior participant, to raise her topic.

The 'fitting' of topics into the conversation at appropriate points can be seen, then, to be a technique involving appreciation of two aspects of the encounter. Firstly, as Schegloff and Sacks point out (1974: 243), a topic must be 'fitted' to a preceding topic, or, if it is not, it must be signalled as 'not fitting' by use of a 'misplacement marker' (1974: 258), a tactic employed by Julie in this example:

ANYWAY . OH I TELL YOU WHAT I WANTED TO ASK YOU....

Secondly, as the above analysis and commentary shows, there are occasions when a topic must also be 'fitted' to an appropriate INTERACTIONAL frame. This second consideration is, in fact, more crucial than 'topical fitting', because, if a suitable topical frame cannot be found or created, the speaker does have the option to mark the topic as 'out of place' by a misplacement marker; no such option is open to a speaker who is unable to find or create a suitable interactional frame.

The tutorial which has provided the data for this discussion has shown, then, that even in the case of primarily transactional encounters, the progress of the conversation is, at times, dependent on the quality of the interaction between the speakers, and that what happens on the interactional level determines, in some cases, what will be talked about at other levels of the discourse.

3.3 Summary

The preceding discussion and exemplification has shown that, in job interviews, the workings of the encounter are inextricably linked to, and dependent upon, the fixed status differential of the participants, but that, in tutorials, although there is a fixed status differential between the participants, expressions of solidarity can be used between the speakers (initiated, of course, by the SUPERIOR participant). When an interactional phase in a tutorial is used to express solidarity rather than status differential, this can pave the way for the introduction of a topic which cannot be raised while the status differential is overtly in operation.

Note that the interactional utterances used throughout all the encounters discussed in this chapter have been status marked, that is, self- or other-oriented (in Laver's terms). None of the encounters has provided examples of what Laver refers to as a 'neutral token'. This is not surprising, as neutral tokens are, according to Laver, used to open encounters between EQUALS, or between non-equals in cases where the status differential is being ignored. As job interviews and tutorials are both kinds of encounter which are trans-actionally dependent on the status differential between the speakers, we would not expect to find such neutral tokens occurring in the dialogue.

The following chapters will examine the workings of interactional dialogue in encounters where status and format are not predetermined, but are liable to variations throughout the discourse, in order to discover the effects these variations may have on the discourse as a whole.

4 Interactional (variable status) encounters

A close examination of variable status encounters (i.e. chats), in which the overall goal is interactional rather than transactional, must be approached in a different way from the study of fixed status encounters (e.g. job interviews). Whereas job interviews have a clearly observable 'event structure', which is designed to progress the dialogue towards the overall transactional goal, and within which the participants act out their appropriate, complementary roles, chats do not have an event structure as such; the structure of the encounter is simply the linguistic reflection of the collection of roles adopted by the speakers in their pursuit of the overall interactional goal.

Because chats lack an overall transactional goal—that is, they have no 'aim' in terms of the outside world—it has been generally assumed that they are without an overall structure of any kind, and there has been no attempt to analyse them at any level higher than the conversational turn. (The ethnomethodologists have dealt with 'sequences' of turns, but, as Chapter 5, section 5.1. will show, their approach has concentrated on what I have termed the PRACTICAL, rather than the INTERACTIONAL management of the encounter.)

The unquestionable unpredictability of conversational topics in chats has added substantially to this assumption, and has resulted in chats being regarded as unsuitable encounter types for macro-analysis because they are 'random' and subject to constant topic shifting. Sinclair and Coulthard are typical of many authorities, e.g. Brown and Yule (1983: 11), Crystal and Davy (1969: 115), when they write: 'In normal conversation . . . changes of topic are unpredictable' (Sinclair and Coulthard 1975: 4).

I do not wish to argue with the view that topics in chats are unpredictable in general, although in Chapter 5 I shall show that particular kinds of topics can be expected to arise in special circumstances which often occur in chats. For the moment, however, I propose to show that, in spite of the general unpredictability of topics in chats, there is nevertheless a loose macro-structure to be observed which is based on the ways speakers present the different topics which are covered in the dialogue.

Inspection of a series of chats—for instance, those which provide the examples for this work—reveals that they are all composed of four different elements, identifiable and distinguishable by the form of their presentation, and also, in some cases, by their position in the dialogue. The occurrence of this macro-structure in all the examples inspected indicates that it is, indeed, a structure common to all such encounters. I have chosen the terms Introduction, Speech-in-action, Story and Closing to refer to these elements, all of which will be exemplified and discussed in detail in subsequent sections. Before going on to such exemplification, however, it is necessary first to give some indication of how such categories are to be understood.

The following detailed discussion will show that these four categories are adequate to describe the interactive structure on which chats are based, and it will further show that this structure is designed so as to allow participants to pursue the interactional goal of the maintenance and development of their interpersonal relationship, in that it provides the opportunity for both (all) participants to exchange evaluations, to make substantial contributions to the conversation, to select topics and sub-topics, and to exchange the complementary roles of superior/inferior throughout the discourse.

4.1 Categories defined

4.1.1 Introduction

I did originally consider borrowing Laver's term 'opening phase' (1975: 217) for this element, but decided against it because Laver's model is based on the implicit assumption that the opening phase differs from the 'medial phase' in the nature of its goal direction. Whereas he views the medial phase (in which the 'main business' of the encounter takes place) as directly concerned with a transactional goal, he views the opening phase as primarily concerned with an interactional goal. This interactional goal is, of course, in his model, ultimately directed towards the transactional end of achieving the 'main business' of the encounter, but its immediate purpose is to set up an interpersonal framework between the speakers.

In chats, which are primarily, and essentially, interactional encounters, there is no 'main business' and, therefore, no 'medial phase' in Laver's sense of the term. I have chosen, therefore, to use a different terminology from Laver, although the term 'Introduction' is still intended to refer, as does Laver's term 'opening phase', to what happens at the beginning of a linguistic encounter.

Introduction can be identified in two ways: firstly (and rather loosely) by its POSITION in the discourse, i.e. it occurs at, or near, the beginning of the discourse and secondly (and more accurately), by its strongly ritualised FORM.

4.1.1.1 *Form of Introduction*

Before discussing specific examples, it is helpful, I think, to consider what might be described as an 'ideal' Introduction, that is, one which any native speaker of English would agree to be, in a notional fashion, 'complete'. Such an Introduction would consist, in a two-speaker conversation, of two utterances each—first, a ritualised greeting from each speaker, such as *good morning*, *hello* etc., depending on the formality of the encounter, and the intimacy of the speakers, followed by a formulaic 'well-wishing'. This feature is very widespread and is to be compared with what Malinowski refers to as 'Inquiries as to health' (1923: 313) from each speaker. The well-wishing may take various forms, again depending on factors such as formality and intimacy—a standard example would be *how are you/fine, how are you*.

This 'set' of greeting/greeting + well-wishing/well-wishing can be regarded as a 'complete' Introduction, a reasonable and predictable opening to an encounter. In practice, however, the Introduction does not always take this form; as the following examples will show, there are frequently occasions of face-to-face dialogue in which Introduction is partially (or occasionally wholly) absent.

4.1.2 Speech-in-action

As Chapter 1, section 1.3.1, explains, Malinowski originally coined this term in 1923, to refer to language which is used 'in connection with vital work' (312), where the utterances are 'embedded in action' and function as 'a link in concerted human activity'. The encounters which are under discussion in this work do not, of course, involve such language use because they do not involve such action. Actions are sometimes performed during these inter-actional encounters, and the speech participants do sometimes refer to these actions, but they cannot, in any sense, be described as 'vital work'—nor do they, in general, involve any kind of 'concerted human activity', such as the fishing expedition which provides Malinowski with his examples. They are, however, similar to the more gross actions described by Malinowski, in that their occurrence in an encounter in part defines the nature of that encounter. Just as the fishing expedition is defined as such by the activities of which it is composed (and the verbal exchanges associated with those activities), so the casual chat between friends is defined as such by activities appropriate to the event, such as offering and accepting gifts and cups of tea (along with the verbal exchanges associated with such actions). The 'activities' which take place in a chat stand, then, in the same relation to the encounter as do the activities which take place in a fishing expedition.

I have, therefore, borrowed the term 'Speech-in-action' for my analysis, as it is the most efficient way of describing the kind of language use I am dealing with in my examples, which is, of course, even in my interactional data, firmly 'embedded in action'.

I have indicated in Chapter 1, section 1.4.3, that the encounters with which I am concerned here, being primarily interactional encounters, can be regarded as occasions of phatic communion. The overall goal of such an encounter is the creation and/or maintenance of social bonds between the speakers. We would not, then, expect to find instances of Speech-in-action (in Malinowski's original sense of the term) in such an encounter—the Speech-in-action which furthers the overall goal of the encounter will be suited to that goal, and, instead of what might be seen as the 'gross' Speech-in- action of a fishing expedition, we would expect to find a much 'reduced' version, suitable to the ongoing 'activity' of a relaxed chat. The various types of Speech-in-action which can be found in chats can, however, be seen to parallel the various 'gross' types described by Malinowski.

The most obvious example of Speech-in-action as Malinowski observed it functioning among the Trobriand Islanders is, of course, in warnings and instructions; a 'low-key' version of these may sometimes be found in chats—one can often hear utterances such as:

> mind, that might be a bit hot,

and

> pass us the ash tray.

In addition to such unambiguously definable examples, however, Malinowski also mentions the kind of Speech-in-action which does not actually FACILITATE the ongoing action, but which is firmly EMBEDDED in it. In the case of the Trobriand Islanders, he refers to the kind of utterance which expresses: 'keenness in the pursuit or impatience at some technical difficulty, joy of achievement or disappointment at failure' (1923: 311), and this too has its parallel in a chat. It is clear that, in the context of a fishing expedition, such utterances are, indeed, firmly embedded in the ongoing action; the ongoing action is the activity of fishing, and speakers refer to that activity by uttering evaluations of various kinds, that is, they comment on the EVENT in which they are involved. In a chat, the event in which the speakers are involved is the event of being together in a social way. This may seem to be a very different kind of event from a fishing expedition in that it may seem to be, in some sense, 'formless', or a 'NON-event'. To take this view would be, however, to assume that transactional encounters involve the participants in a more positive way (in terms of their DELIBERATE participation) than do interactional encounters, but this view has been more than adequately exploded by Goffman. He distinguishes between a 'co-participant in an encounter' and 'someone reckoned simply as present in a setting or a social occasion' (1971: 27), and the detailed discussions throughout his work establish that social contact of any kind (including a chat) is very much a matter for conscious and deliberate participation by an individual who CHOOSES to become part of an encounter.

A chat is, then, an encounter involving the 'deliberate' participation of the speakers/actors in the same way as is a fishing expedition, and the 'activity' in which the speakers are participating is the 'activity' of being TOGETHER. No 'gross action' is involved in this, but this fact does not preclude the participants from commenting on their joint 'activity'. They will, in fact, frequently comment on various aspects of the encounter, sometimes (particularly in the case of a meeting between close friends who have not met for a lengthy period) making overt reference to the social contact itself—*oh it is nice to see you*—but, more often, exchanging evaluations of various factors in their immediate environment. These comments on the immediate environment may refer to the general environment as it affects both participants (e.g. *what terrible weather*), or they may be specifically directed by one speaker towards the person or property of his/her co-conversationalist (e.g. *I like your carpet*, *see you've got a new hi-fi*, *you've had your hair done*). All such comments can, in the context of an interaction, be seen as firmly embedded in the ongoing 'action', and can, therefore, be categorised as Speech-in-action.

Utterances which are classified as Speech-in-action in the subsequent examples are, then, those which refer to the immediate environment of the speakers. It should be noted that this 'immediate environment' has three aspects:

1. Temporal
Speech-in-action must be embedded in the current, ongoing action of the encounter, so that a reference to how the roses in the garden look NOW would be Speech-in-action, whereas an utterance about what the storm did to the roses last week would not. Such an utterance would, in fact, be a story, or part of a story (see section 4.1.3 below). Although the temporal aspect of Speech-in-action is extremely restricted (i.e. 'now'), it need not be made verbally explicit in the utterance, and, indeed, is not usually made so. This temporal restriction is, however, an essential component of Speech-in-action—it must be present for an utterance to be classified as Speech-in-action, combined with one (or both) of the other two aspects.

2. Physical
This includes all objects and conditions which are currently physically observable by the speakers, such as the weather, natural features such as plants and scenery, any artefacts which may be present, non-human animate beings such as pet cats, and, of course, the speakers themselves.

3. Social

This includes any comments about the encounter itself. It must, as I have already pointed out, be combined with the temporal restriction of Speech-in-action to be so classified. Closing utterances (see section 4.1.4 below) often involve comments about the encounter, but differ from Speech-in-action in their temporal location.

4.1.3 Story

Story accounts for most of the time spent by the participants in informal conversational encounters (compare length of Story examples with all other examples, this chapter, sections 4.2.1–4.2.4 inclusive). For this particular element, I originally considered using Malinowski's term 'narrative', but found it to be inappropriate because the narrative identified and described by Malinowski is very much an 'institutionalised' form of story-telling, i.e. a formal entertainment, in which one speaker has the right and the duty to tell a story, and the other participant has the right and the duty to be the audience. This concept of the narrative does not cover the more informal kind of story-telling which occurs interactively in casual conversation. My category is designed to include not only formal narratives but also (and more crucially for my discussion) the more informal kind of story-telling, so I have used the general term 'Story'.

This term has been used by a number of other writers, but they have tended to use the term in a way which excludes many of the stretches of conversation which I regard as stories. De Beaugrande, for instance (1982), refers to 'problem-solving' as an essential factor in a story; similarly, Stein (1982) regards 'goal-based' action as an essential; and both writers rely heavily for their argumentation on the extent to which texts are REGARDED AS STORIES by sample 'audiences' (particularly pupils and teachers). To ask any 'audience' whether a specific text is or is not a 'proper' story is, of course, in some way to 'load the question'. Any individual who is asked such a question will undoubtedly make the assumption that he/she is being asked to identify a particular KIND of story, i.e. one which is culturally recognised as such, one which can be classified in some way as 'an entertainment'. To answer the question must, then, involve the individual in some degree of decision-making about HOW FAR the text is entertaining, and this must ultimately come down to a judgement by the individual of how much he/she LIKES the text/story, and such a judgement is clearly a red herring in any discussion of what is, or is not, a story.

It is true, of course, that the term 'story' as generally understood does involve entertainment, and this kind of story-telling does occur in casual conversation. The use I make of the term in this work is not intended to exclude such stories, but I also wish to include the less obvious kinds of stories, as they make up so much of what happens in linguistic interactions.

One definition of a story which is useful to my analysis is that given by Prince (1973), who proposes that a text can be considered to be a story if it contains at least one event, which arises out of a particular state: the event must result in a state different from the original. According to Prince, it is not necessary to have any animate actor involved in this process—a change in state in the physical world is sufficient, so that, according to this definition, a sequence such as:

> the pond was frozen, then the sun came out and it thawed

would be classified as a story.

I would agree with Prince that a sequence such as this, involving a STATE, an EVENT and a new STATE is, indeed, sufficient for a text to be considered as a story. Inspection of the various corpora which provide the examples for this work reveals, however, that in practice speakers tell stories about ANIMATE (usually human) participants, and that, in the telling of these stories, the participants are invariably specified. The corpora further indicate that speakers also include two other factors in their stories, temporal location and evaluation. Temporal location is usually explicitly referred to in the text, e.g. *last week*, *the other day*; when it is not explicitly stated, it is implicit in the context—an example of this kind of implied and understood temporal location can be found in Example (22) (this chapter).

The second factor which appears to occur in some form in all stories is EVALUATION (a point also noted by Labov (1972: 366–75)). Again, this is usually made explicit by the speaker, e.g. *oh it was really terrible*, although the lexical items which occur in some stories are already heavily evaluatively loaded and require no separate statement of evaluation (see Example (26), this chapter).

Stories in my analysis are, then, classified as such if the stretch of speech in question includes four factors:

1. a coherent sequence of state–event–state;
2. specification of participants;
3. temporal location;
4. evaluation.

It should be noted here that the writers who have studied the telling of stories (including those whose work has been referred to above) have concentrated exclusively on stories which are told as a monologue. Such stories do occur in dialogue, and the corpora which provide the basis for my comments here include several examples of such stories. The bulk of stories which occur in interactions are, however, essentially dialogic—that is, they are told not through one long conversational turn taken by the 'story-teller', but through a series of short turns by both 'teller' and 'audience', often with the 'audience' providing questions to elicit more information, and sometimes even with the 'audience' PROVIDING some of the information, in the form of guesses—one part of the story frequently provided by the 'audience' being evaluation, which may be inserted at various points throughout the story. This dialogic form of story telling means that the distinction between 'story-teller' and 'audience' becomes blurred, because what is happening in such a situation is that the speakers are collaborating in a story-telling.

One last point should be made here before leaving this section. In my analysis, I show sometimes very long stretches of the dialogue as 'Story'. This does not mean that the speakers are involved in the telling of only one story throughout this section—they may sometimes tell a series of stories—but until they move on to some other element, such as 'Speech-in-action', they are still in what can be considered as 'Story MODE'. So, throughout this discussion, STORY refers to the discourse element 'Story', and STORY refers to the topically bound actual stories which occur while this element is in progress.

4.1.4 Closing

Closings would appear, in theory, to be largely characterised by formulaic utterances. One imagines a typical Closing to take the following form (or something very similar):

A: I must go, it's been lovely to see you, see you again soon.
B: Thanks for coming, it's been lovely, see you soon.
A: Bye.
B: Bye.

involving the use of repeated items, references back to the quality of the terminating encounter, and references forward to future meetings.

Laver (1975) shows that actual Closings do, in fact, follow this imagined form. He describes, in some detail, how the repetition, the positive evaluations of the terminating encounter and the references to potential future meetings all serve both to consolidate the relationship which has been developed throughout the encounter, and to present the encounter as part of a wider social network of similar encounters involving further development of the relationship.

The corpora which provide the data for this work contain few examples of Closings (for further comments on this see section 4.2.4 below), but observation of encounters in general does indicate that the format described by Laver is, indeed, typical of Closings.

4.2 Analysis of interactions with examples

4.2.1 Examples of Introduction

When considering occasions of disturbance of the 'ideal' pattern of this element, it should be borne in mind that there are likely to be differences between face-to-face interactions and those which take place by telephone, due to the need which arises in telephone encounters for the participants to use speech for identification purposes. This need means that speakers are more likely to use a conventional, formulaic opening, together with a formal announcement of the identity of the caller. It is, perhaps, the formal constraint on the caller of having to identify himself which leads both participants to resort to the formality of a strictly patterned, formulaic opening. However, even in telephone encounters, where the voices of the participants are very well known to one another, and there is no need for any formal identification, it appears that openings of telephone encounters have a greater tendency to be stereotypical than the openings of face-to-face encounters. It is, however, by no means certain that such telephone openings will be stereotypical, and observation of actual instances reveals that participants have, and take advantage of, far greater choice in this matter than one might assume from a purely intuitive consideration of this area of interaction. Nevertheless, the fact remains that the openings of telephone interactions tend to be rather more in line with the basic 'complete' format of the element Introduction than do other interactions. I shall, therefore, treat these two areas separately, dealing first with the telephone interactions, as they seem, in general, to have closer links with the formulaic pattern which is the basis of the element Introduction as set out above, and I shall go on to discuss and exemplify the first element which occurs in face-to-face interactions.

4.2.1.1 *Telephone interactions*

Example (1) Jefferson's tape—NB:II:3:R
        INTRODUCTION
Lottie: ....lo
Emma: g'morning Letitia
Lottie: u-h how'r you
Emma: fine how'r *you*
        STORY
Lottie: *eh heh* heh wudiyih know
Emma: hhh jis got down last night eh (etc.)

In this example, the element occurs in the form of the basic pattern, with the exchange of formulaic greetings followed by the exchange of formulaic tokens expressing concern about health and well-being. Exactly how formulaic and ritualised these tokens are is clear from the way the second part of the second exchange is not treated as a question—Lottie simply accepts it as the proper, formulaic response to her first part. She does not even wait to hear it through, but overlaps Emma's utterance with a movement straight on to another element—in this case, Story. This is not to suggest that Lottie's utterance after the two opening exchanges is itself a story, but it provides a story slot, which Emma then takes up, and proceeds with, encouraged by Lottie, over the next few utterances.

Some other examples will show how the basic pattern of the element can be disturbed.

Example (2) Jefferson's tape—NB:I:6:R
      INTRODUCTION
Lottie: hello
Emma: good morning
Lottie: how'r you
Emma: oh hi honey
      STORY
      we haven' gotten together have we
Lottie: oh gosh no let's see . Thursday night I went it town I came back
      Friday it wz late (etc.)

In this example, the caller speaks first and clearly has to complete two utterances before the second speaker can identify her. The ritualistic *how'r you* is used by the second speaker purely as a clue to the caller's identity, and the formulaic question is never answered. Instead, the second speaker produces a greeting as a response to it. She has, in her first utterance, already greeted the caller, but with a very formal *good morning*; on learning the caller's identity, she produces another greeting, this time a much more informal one accompanied by a familiar address term, *oh hi honey*, which is obviously more appropriate for the relationship which exists between the speakers. In effect, then, the second speaker restarts the interaction by an informal, intimate opening, completely ignores the *how'r you* formula, and goes straight on to introduce another element, again, as in the previous example, producing what Lottie interprets and employs as a story slot.

Example (3) Jefferson's tape—NB:IV:II:R
      INTRODUCTION
Gladys: hhhel*lo*
Emma: *t h* I'd like tuh wish you a happy Thanksgiving fr'm Balboa
Gladys: oh thank you dee*ah*
Emma: *ihh* hhe:nh he::: +ah+
Gladys: +hnh+
      STORY

Emma: ah didju *getcher* paper this: morning
Gladys: *ahshh*
Emma: it wz ou:t'n +fron'v+
Gladys: +m+
Emma: a:r place
Gladys: yes dear ah di:d (etc.)

Here, Gladys's first utterance is clearly taken by Emma simply to signal that Gladys is available to talk to—she does not treat it as a greeting because she does not respond with any similar token. Instead, her first utterance is a special form of ritualised enquiry about well-being—in this case it is an expression of well-wishing with particular reference to *Thanksgiving*. Such well-wishings are, of course, also formulaic, but, presumably because it is a token used on only one day a year, it does not always produce an identical token as a response, as in this case, where Gladys does not return the well-wishing, but simply thanks Emma for it. Emma then provides, as in Examples (1) and (2), a Story slot, and the Story element takes over for the next four utterances.

Example (4) Jefferson's tape—NB:II:5:R
      INTRODUCTION
Lottie: hello:
      STORY
Emma: are you answering the pho::ne (SMILE VOICE)
Lottie: ehh hhah hh I wz j's gunnuh ca:ll yuh ehh *huh huh*
Emma: *I jis* go:t he:re hh (etc.)

In this example, the answerer begins with the usual *hello*, but the introductory phase does not proceed beyond this; instead, the caller provides a Story slot immediately—it is, presumably, unusual for Lottie to answer the phone. Lottie then gives a very truncated version of a story, but this does not become expanded by either speaker—instead, Emma begins to tell another story, which then proceeds over the next few utterances. Lottie's *hello* in this example is clearly not regarded (at least by Emma) as properly part of an introductory phase at all. She treats it purely as a signal that Lottie can hear her, and immediately moves on to the story element, and Lottie is quite clearly happy to go along with this, so that neither speaker treats this as at all deviant.

4.2.1.1.1 *Comments on telephone interactions*
In telephone interactions, then, while Introduction in its full form can occur, it is not an obligatory part of the encounter because there are many cases where the relationship between the participants is such that this element can be dispensed with. When Introduction does occur, it rarely appears in its 'full'

form. In Jefferson's corpus there are twelve telephone conversations which include openings—of these only one has a full Introduction (see Example (1) above). This is not, of course, to suggest that participants who share a close relationship may not use the full introductory element as the opening phase of the encounter—but they are not obliged to. As the above examples show, the initial greeting may be simply interpreted as a signal that the answerer is available to talk to, in which case it should not properly be regarded as part of Introduction at all, as it is operating as the second part of a summons–answer sequence, the first part being the ringing of the telephone. Ritualistic well-wishings may or may not be exchanged, or only one of the speakers may deliver a token of this kind. Whatever disturbances in the basic pattern of the element may occur, speakers treat this as normal, so even in telephone interactions, Introduction is, to a large extent, an optional part of the encounter. In face-to-face encounters, which do not have the problems of how to signal speaker identity and speaker availability, one would expect to find even more cases of pattern disruption. A close inspection of transcribed data from such interactions will show whether this is indeed the case.

4.2.1.2 *Face-to-face interactions*

Example (5) Tape—Dawsons
         STORY
Catherine: *did you get lost +then*+
         INTRODUCTION
Geoff: *hello*
Chris: +(laugh)+ *(laugh)*
         STORY
Geoff: *no we didn't* what we did however encounter was an accident on +the road+
Catherine: +ooooohhh+ - not to you
Geoff: oh no no no no - (inaud.) there were thousands of cars (etc.)

In this example, Geoff, who is an incomer, begins by delivering the first token of an Introduction. At the same time, however, Catherine, the hostess, asks him for a story, which he immediately begins to give, so that all parties move straight on to Story.

Example (6) London–Lund Corpus Tape—S.2.7.
      INTRODUCTION
a: *hello*
C: *hello*
      SPEECH-IN-ACTION
      sorry I'm late
a: *(laugh) that's alright* are you

b: *(laugh,murmur)*
C: yes . I said half past seven (etc.)
a: oh I expected you between about -. half past and quarter to
     INTRODUCTION
C: hello Liz
     SPEECH-IN-ACTION
     sorry I'm late (laugh)
b: oh I like your hair
C: m
a: yes Ann you've had it curled
C: jiz . (laugh)
a: yes that's nice - I say that's nice

Here, only the first tokens of Introduction are exchanged—the greetings; there are no well-wishings. Instead, the incomer's lateness is put up for discussion, so that the speakers move into Speech-in-action, although the incomer, C, does deliver another introductory greeting token (to speaker b) later on. After this, the participants move straight on to Speech-in-action again, when the incomer receives positive evaluation on her hairstyle.

Example (7) Tape—Celia
          SPEECH-IN-ACTION
Celia: nous sommes ici
Chris: mon chateau
Celia: aaa hh (gasp) you're blonde again
          STORY
Chris: (inaud.) the sun
Celia: (inaud.)
Chris: no it's true cause I put a light brown on it and every time I go in the
          sun and wash it it goes another shade blonder and then I do it again
          with the light brown and six weeks later I'm a blonde again I mean
          it's just sitting in the sun - the colour's fugitive *(inaud.)*
          SPEECH-IN-ACTION
Louise: *where's Lucy*
Chris: she oh no əm . Lu -- Lu - go up there - and there's a door on the right
          - go in there . she can't hear cause she's got her . tape on --- go on that
          one
Celia: (inaud.)
Chris: go on go in
(NOISE OF CHILDREN SQUEALING)
Celia: (laugh)
Chris: (inaud.)
Celia: looks awfully nice
Chris: looks better than the last time you saw it (etc.)

I have quoted from this tape at some length in order to show that at no time do the adult participants in this encounter make any attempt to create an Introduction. Instead, they use Speech-in-action and Story. It should be noted that the second occurrence of Speech-in-action involves primarily not the two adult participants, but one of the adults and the visiting children—so this section is, in fact, in terms of the main flow of the interaction, an aside. It does not, furthermore, become woven into the mainstream of the interaction by the adult participants, because, once the children have left the immediate scene of the interaction, the adults do not refer to this passage again; it can, then, be disregarded as it does not form part of the structure of the main interaction.

Example (8) Tape—Dresses
   SPEECH-IN-ACTION
K: (inaud.) energy
C: (inaud.) washing up
   STORY
K: so what did I do this morning then start painting the skirting board white and when I opened (etc.)

In this example, after a brief exchange of Speech-in-action tokens, the incomer begins a story. She does this by providing a story slot, i.e. asking a question, *so what did I do this morning then*, and then answering that question by a story. Both participants then proceed with Story for some time.

Example (9) Tape—Xmas 83
(KNOCK ON DOOR)
   SPEECH-IN-ACTION
K: *before I forget*
   STORY
C: *ah I was just about to phone you
   SPEECH-IN-ACTION
K: before I forget I'm gonna do it this moment ---
C: oh my key . yes . give me it back . give me back my key --
   STORY
K: why . were you gonna phone me and say don't come
C: no I was gonna phone you and say aren't *you coming*
   SPEECH-IN-ACTION
K: *oh yes* sorry about that (laugh)
C: (inaud.)
K: sorry about that
C: look I've just moved my chair to the phone -
   STORY
   *was just about to

K: *oh you thought you* were gonna have a long k I see (laugh)
C: I was gonna listen to the excuses ---
K: oh -----
(SHE HANDS KEY BACK)
    SPEECH-IN-ACTION
C: thank you dear
    STORY
K: did you get a Christmas card from us
C: yes thank you
K: oh—I looked was looking for it everywhere (etc.)

This encounter begins with a long phase of Speech-in-action overlapping with Story, where both speakers provide a topic, and both topics are dealt with together. After this, K, the incomer, provides a story slot by the question *did you get a Christmas card from us*. This slot is not, however, designed to be filled by the next speaker—the question is clearly designed to be an introduction for K to tell the story, which, with the collaboration of the other speaker, she proceeds to do.

It is clear from the above examples that, as expected in face-to-face interactions, Introduction is very frequently partially or wholly omitted, and such encounters often open with other elements. It will now be useful to summarise the analyses of the examples in this section and in section 4.2.1.1 above to see if any general conclusions may be drawn about the occurrence of Introduction as an opening phase in telephone and in face-to-face interactions.

4.2.1.3 *Conclusions about the occurrence of Introduction*

In the examples of opening phases given in the preceding sections, of the four telephone examples only one opens with a 'full' Introduction—that is an exchange of greeting tokens and an exchange of enquiries about well-being (this example is, as I have said in section 4.2.1.1.1 above, unique in Jefferson's corpus; the other three show only a partial Introduction, Example (4) having only one greeting token, which is not reciprocated. Of the five face-to-face examples only two open with an Introduction of any kind, and none has the full set of greeting/greeting, + well-wishing/well-wishing.

This difference between opening phases in telephone and face-to-face interactions is evident throughout the data at my disposal; out of twelve transcribed telephone interactions (Jefferson's corpus) all twelve opened with some kind of Introduction. Out of a total of eight face-to-face interactions examined (including those discussed above) four open with an Introduction, of which only one is a 'full' Introduction; the other four all open with Speech-in-action. These findings indicate that Introduction is, indeed, more likely to occur in telephone interactions than in face-to-face interactions.

A further fact has emerged from this analysis; that those interactions which do not open with Introduction do open with Speech-in-action, and this seems to indicate that speakers regard Speech-in-action as a suitable and normal opening for interaction.

4.2.1.4 *Laver's model and Introductions*

As I have already mentioned in section 1.4.1 above, Laver's 1975 article deals largely with the opening phases of encounters. As an 'opening phase' frequently consists of, or contains, an Introduction, the following sections will examine the Introductions I have already discussed in this'chapter in the light of Laver's comments on opening phases.

As the examples in the following section will be taken from the interactive data (which consists of encounters between solidary equals), it is reasonable to suppose that there will be a number of neutral opening remarks, as, if Laver is correct, this is a choice frequently made by equals opening an encounter. There will also, presumably, be examples of self- and other-oriented openers, as the participants in the interactions do, in all cases, share a solidary relationship, and have therefore, according to Laver, access to a free choice of opener.

Before beginning a discussion of examples, it should be noted that Laver's references to 'opening remarks' must not be taken too literally, as greetings are excluded from the discussion, which, in fact, only covers remarks 'Apart from formulaic greetings' (1975: 222).

The following examples will therefore illustrate those opening remarks which occur in the interactive data at my disposal, but will ignore any greeting tokens which are also present in the discourse.

4.2.1.5 *Examples*

I shall in this section use only the first two utterances of each encounter in order to concentrate on the actual opening words used by each speaker.

In spite of Laver's detailed comments, it is rather difficult to decide on a criterion for self- or other-orientation. Laver's examples of *hot work this*, and *that looks like hot work*, seem to indicate that the decision should be made on the basis of which speaker (or which speaker's activity) is commented upon, so this is how I shall distinguish them.

Example (10) Tape—Dresses
(NOISE OF HOST WASHING UP)
Incomer: (inaud.) energy
Host: (inaud.) washing up

Although much of this first exchange is inaudible, due to the noise of dishes clattering, it seems plausible that the first utterance is designed to be an other-oriented remark, and the second utterance is obviously a self-oriented remark.

Example (11) Tape—Dawsons
Incomer: *hello*
Host: *did you get lost then*
Incomer: no we didn't what we did however encounter was an accident on the road

Here, the first remark is clearly other-oriented, being totally concerned with the actions of the hearer; the second remark is a self-oriented token, but it should be noted in this case that the Incomer does NOT have a free choice of token here—he is asked to tell a story about what happened to him, and he proceeds to do this, inevitably beginning with a self-oriented token.

Example (12) Tape—Celia
Incomer: nous sommes ici
Host: mon chateau

Here, both opening utterances are self-oriented. This is rather an interesting exchange, because the two opening remarks appear to have no connection—both have, as their focus of attention, the psychological world of the speaker. In this case, however, the speakers are signalling close solidarity by their use of French, as the interaction took place in England, between two English speakers who were not in the presence of any French speakers—so these speakers have chosen to use French as a register showing solidarity, regardless of their different choice of subject matter, and their apparent absorption with their discrete psychological worlds.

Example (13) London–Lund Corpus Tape—S.1.4
Host: Richard hallo . I've just *s set out*
Incomer: *thank you*

The first speaker here begins with a greeting preceded by a vocative, and this appears to transform the greeting into an other-oriented token. The next part of the utterance is an incomplete sentence, but is clearly designed as a self-oriented token, so the first speaker in this example has used two tokens in his first utterance—one other-oriented and one self-oriented. The second speaker's utterance is a ritualised thanking and is, therefore, an other-oriented token.

Example (14) Tape—John
Host: oh . come in John . oh . I got cramp -- ohhh . want a glass of beer
Incomer: thought you'd never ask

The first speaker in this example begins with an other-oriented token, *come in*, which, like the previous example, is accompanied by a vocative. In this case, the addition of the vocative gives even more force to the other-orientation of the remark. Next comes a self-oriented remark, and this is then followed by another other-oriented remark. The second speaker responds directly to the last part of the first speaker's utterance with a return of an other-oriented remark.

Example (15) London–Lund Corpus Tape—S.2.7
Host: *hello*
Incomer: *hello* . sorry I'm late
Host: . (laughs) that's alright are you -

This, opening (after the greetings) with *sorry I'm late*, is a rather problematic example, because it is impossible to classify according to Laver's analysis. In one way it can be seen as a self-oriented remark, being concerned with the action of the speaker, but the word *sorry* (showing concern for the HEARER) is quite clearly an other-oriented signal. This seems, then, to fall into a category outside those mentioned by Laver—it is certainly not neutral, and yet it has characteristics of both self- and other-orientation. It is, I think, best described as a shared world token, as it functions to make the action of the speaker part of the hearer's private world. In one sense, of course, all self-oriented remarks which are addressed to a hearer are designed to do this—otherwise the speaker would not offer such remarks. But in cases like this particular example, this is made linguistically explicit by use of a token like *sorry*, which, like *thank you*, is always an other-orientation signal, together with explicit reference to the speaker's action, '*I'M late*.

   The second 'opening' utterance in this example is clearly an other-oriented token, which, in this case, is topically bound to the preceding utterance.

Example (16) Tape—Xmas 83
Incomer: *before I forget*
Host: *ah I was just about to phone you*

This is a similar example to (15) above. The first speaker, although producing only an incomplete sentence, is clearly embarking on a self-oriented remark. The second speaker, however, again, as in Example (15), delivers what can only be described as a shared world token: '*I was just about to phone YOU*.

Example (17) London–Lund Corpus Tape—S.1.9
1st speaker: Geoffrey Ramsden *how are you*
2nd speaker: *oh hello* I've been longing to see you how are you

Due to the accessibility of the transcription only for this example, the original audio tape being unavailable because of restrictions arising out of the surreptitious nature of the recording, it is difficult to decide, in this case, which speaker is the host and which the incomer. For the same reason, it is impossible to decide whether the first part of the first utterance: *Geoffrey Ramsden* is a vocative and, therefore, an other-oriented remark, or a self-identification, and, therefore, self-oriented. The second part of the first utterance, however, *how are you*, is unambiguously other-oriented. The second speaker's utterance has two different tokens—first, another example of a shared world token: '*I've been longing to see* YOU, and second: *how are you*—a clear, other-oriented token.

4.2.1.6 *Commentary on examples*

As the preceding examples illustrate, the speakers in these interactions do, as Laver claims, have a free choice of opener. There are three points, however, which are evident from the examples, which contradict some of Laver's conclusions. Firstly, speakers are not, as Laver's article implies, constrained to choose only one token as an opener. Example (17) shows that speakers may, without a pause to separate them, string together up to three different kinds of openers within the same utterance. While it may be possible to argue that Laver does not intend the expression 'opening remark' to mean necessarily the same as 'opening utterance', and the pauses which have been transcribed in Examples (13), (14), and (15) can be seen as boundaries between opening remarks and subsequent remarks within the same utterance, the lack of pauses in Example (17), and its undoubted inclusion of three different kinds of token, show that, FOR THE SPEAKER, this is ONE opener, made up of three different kinds of token. Given this, it seems likely that the other examples, which show the use of a variety of different tokens within one utterance are also to be regarded as single openers made up of different parts. As in all cases, except Example (14), the pauses are of short duration (indicated by [.] in the transcription). The one exception (example (14)), which contains a long pause [--] between the second and third tokens, may possibly be an example of a speaker producing an opener and a subsequent remark within one utterance, although as this particular example is from an interaction where the first speaker was suffering from cramp and expressing pain by words and gestures during the long pause, even this argument seems rather unlikely. It seems, then, more reasonable to suggest that an opening remark can be taken to be the same as an opening utterance, and that opening remarks are not, as Laver implies, necessarily restricted to the choice of one kind of token.

The second point is that, although speakers do appear to have a free choice of opener, there are no examples of neutral tokens used as openers, although Laver claims that these are frequently used to open encounters between social equals.

The third point is the evidence, in Examples (15), (16) and (17), for the existence of a category different from, and additional to those given by

Laver—shared world tokens. It is rather surprising that Laver does not include these in his comments, as much of the drift of his discussion is concerned with the need speech participants feel to create a 'momentary solidarity' in order to allow them to interact at all. This means that they are attempting to CREATE a shared world of some sort, within which they can communicate for the duration of the encounter. As this is the case, the option of a shared world token as an opener, or as part of an opener, seems a reasonable thing to expect, as it is the most explicit way of setting up such a framework for communication.

To summarise, then, Laver's article does raise some useful points, by differentiating between various kinds of openers and showing how these can be related to different status patterns between speakers. There is, however, as the preceding paragraphs and examples show, rather more to opening remarks than Laver acknowledges.

As I have already mentioned, Laver categorises the examples he uses as phatic communion, but, as I have pointed out in section 1.4.3, Malinowski's original definition of phatic communion relates to far more than simply the opening and closing phases of an encounter; in the case of an interaction, it relates, in fact, to the whole encounter. The examples given and discussed by Laver in 1975 cannot, in my terms (nor, indeed, in Malinowski's terms) be regarded as phatic communion—they relate, in all cases, to the immediate environment of the speakers and should, therefore, be categorised instead as Speech-in-action.

4.2.2 Examples of Speech-in-action

The varieties of Speech-in-action referred to in section 4.1.2 above are realised in various ways throughout the corpora, for example:

Physical aspect

Example (18) Tape—Dawsons

would you like a glass or we've got some fizzy red

Example (19) Tape—Dresses

oh I haven't ev I've even got my slippers on how disgusting never mind

Example (20) Tape—Celia

that's caught a bit actually

Social aspect

Example (21) London–Lund Corpus Tape—S.2.7

sorry I'm late

The way in which Speech-in-action functions in interaction, and the various forms it may take, will become clearer in the following section, dealing with Story, an element which appears to be closely connected with Speech-in-action.

4.2.3 Examples of Story

Out of the twenty interactions (twelve telephone and eight face-to-face) for which I have transcriptions which include the opening phase, eleven have a Story as the second element (eight of the telephone interactions and three of the face-to-face interactions). It appears, then, that Story is the most likely element to occur in second place in interactions, and this is probably because the element Story occurs with such frequency throughout interaction.

Story, then, is a very important element in interaction, and I shall now examine some of the examples which occur in my interactive data.

Example (22) Tape—Dawsons
           INTRODUCTION
Geoff: hello
           STORY
Catherine: *did you get lost then*
Chris: *(laugh)* +(laugh)+
Geoff: +no we didn't+ what we did however encounter was an accident on the *road*
Catherine: *ooohhh*—not to you
Geoff: oh no no no no—(inaud.) there were thousands of cars sort of piled up sort of miles back on the road that goes from Watford to
Catherine: ooohhh
Geoff: St. Albans
Catherine: oh my God
Geoff: (inaud.)
GEOFF OFFERS BOTTLE OF WINE
           SPEECH-IN-ACTION
Catherine: how nice (etc.)

This example begins with a question which opens the way for a story, which is told by Geoff. I have said, in section 4.1.3, that for an event or an action to be related as a story, certain factors must be present in the text—there must be a sequence of state–event–state, and there must be some kind of temporal location. In this case (which involves animate actors and also therefore, specifies WHICH actors are involved—*we*), there is no explicit reference to temporal location. The temporal location is, instead, implicit in the context and the co-text; the story slot *did you get lost then*, which is provided as the host opens the door to the incomers, implies the temporal location of *during your journey here* (i.e. within the last hour). This implication is understood by all parties to the interaction, and so no further temporal location is needed.

It should be noted that the word *then* in *did you get lost then* is nothing to do with temporal location. It does not mean *then* in time (which would be roughly paraphrasable by *next*); it is an informal tag, which is typically used with questions which are EXPECTED to be asked, because both the questioner and the potential answerer are aware that a particular activity or event is of interest to both of them. Even though the questioner has not been involved personally, he expects a report on the action, and the use of *then* signals to the answerer that he should expect to provide such a report.

It should be noted that this question puts great pressure on the hearer to answer with a story. The hearer of:

> did you get lost then

has little choice of whether or not to answer with a story—a simple *yes* or *no* will not suffice. In such a case, the Story slot is set up by the questioner, and the answerer is pressurised to provide a particular story.

This particular example illustrates the dialogic nature of so many of the stories which are told in interactions. It opens with the Story slot question from the host:

> did you get lost then

and the incomer then follows with a story about what delayed them on their way to the host's house. Immediately he begins to tell his story:

> what we did however encounter was an accident on the road

(which, incidentally, contains an implicit negative evaluation in the 'loaded' lexical item *accident*), he is interrupted by the host, who 'joins in' the telling with, first, an evaluation:

> ooohhh,

and then a question to elicit more information:

> not to you.

The incomer (Geoff) then takes another turn, in which he answers this question, and goes on to describe the way in which the *accident* affected him and his passenger:

> there were thousands of cars sort of piled up sort of miles back on the road
> that goes from Watford to.

At this point, the host (Catherine) again takes a turn, providing another evaluation:

ooohhh,

after which Geoff completes his syntactic unit. This is then followed by a final evaluation from Catherine:

oh my God.

Geoff's next turn is inaudible, but I have included it in the section labelled 'Story' because of the widespread tendency of topical sequences (of which this story is an example) to terminate with an inaudible murmur from one of the co-conversationalists (see, for instance, Example (24), this chapter).

Example (23) Tape—Xmas 83
    STORY
K: [1]did you get a Christmas card from us
C: yes thank you
K: oh - I looked was looking for it everywhere this morning . cause Alec's got the . the pile for hand delivery - and my God and I bought that special and I knew you'd forget the joke ---
C: I can't remember the card *yes peas on earth*
K: *peas on earth* did you remember it did you . no you wouldn't
C: no
K: [2]you know that night we went to the Chinese restaurant don't you
C: (inaud.)
K: this əm for some reason it sticks in my mind we had this conversation about peas - and I saw that the very next day I thought kor I'll get that
C: (laugh)
K: and it cause they'll never remember it *cause we'd forgotten already*
C: *couldn't remember (laugh)* oh I couldn't remember it .
    SPEECH-IN-ACTION
    there's there's your card . that's for the kids

As in Example 22, this story begins with a question:

did you get a Christmas card from us.

However, whereas in Example (22), the answer to the opening question becomes the story, in this case the story is told by the questioner, so that the opening question here does not operate as an invitation to the answerer to tell a story, it operates as an introduction to the questioner's own story.

Example (23) illustrates how a Story element may contain more than one story. This contains two (indicated in the above extract by the superscripts 1 and 2); the first is about K's attempts to find the Christmas card, and the message on it (note the explicit reference to temporal location):

I looked was looking for it everywhere this morning.

The second story is related to the first—it takes the listener back in time and gives the reason for K's selection of that particular card. Again she makes an explicit reference to the temporal location:

> that night we went to the Chinese restaurant.

This Story is less dialogic than that in Example (24)—the listener's turns are generally minimal.

Examples (22) and (23) also differ in the way the Stories end; (22) ends with an evaluation by the hearer:

> oh my God

and an inaudible remark by the teller, which seems to signal that he has run out of steam on the story; and (23) ends with a recompletion (see also Chapter 5, p. 96) by the hearer:

> couldn't remember (laugh) oh I couldn't remember it

which is a rather more positive signal that the speaker has nothing more to say on the subject and does not wish to continue it. Both examples move straight from Story into Speech-in-action, and, in both cases, the Speech-in-action concerns gifts being offered—in (22) it is a bottle of wine, and in (23) it is a Christmas card and some presents. This is not unusual, as both these examples are from very early on in the interactions, and, of course, if gifts are to be offered in an interaction, it is likely that they will be offered very near the beginning of the encounter. It is interesting, though, that the gifts are not offered at the opening of the interaction—instead, they are, in both cases, offered after the first occurrence of Story.

Example (24) Tape—Dresses

        STORY

K: so what did I do this morning then [1] start painting the skirting board white and when I opened the tin it weren't white was it was yellow says brilliant white on the pro

C: you're kidding what the wrong colour

K: the wrong colour inside the tin I don't ever remember that happening

C: never ever known that *before*

K: *no*

        SPEECH-IN-ACTION

        oh sorry darling

        STORY

        yeh

C: crazy

K: I couldn't help but laugh [2] I mean you know *me decorate*

C: [1]*well you* think it's your eyes don't you

K: [2] you know me decorate it's taken me twelve years to actually admit
          that I will do some and the first thing I go to do .

C: [1]it's silly

K and C: (laugh)

C: and it really said brilliant white on the outside

K: yeh - Kelly said to me look Mum it's the wrong colour in that tin
          cause there was a little drip on the outside and I said oh no what's
          happened they've put other ones on top . cause it didn't look as
          though it dripped from from the in it wasn't in the rim it was just on
          the outside you know

C: that's ridiculous

K: yeh . [3] so I just said to *(inaud.)*

C: [1] *must* have been a whole batch

K: [3] I said I bought this yesterday and (inaud.) it ain't (laugh) oh . oh
          said I'm terri I said it's not your fault he said I'm afraid we go by
          what's on the tin I said well of course you go by what's on the *tin*

C: *nobody* expects them to open each +one+

K: +they+ expect to open ea

C: God

K: but ə

C: must be the whole batch

K: well he he gave me the next one and I said I think perhaps we'll
          open it . first it's cause only from you know up here Dearman's

C: yeh

K: *(inaud.)*
          SPEECH-IN-ACTION

C: *I've got some stuff to show you*

Again, this example begins with a question, but in this case the questioner
does not wait for an answer, she continues talking by telling her story. This
tactic seems to indicate how common it is for stories to be told as answers to
questions, so that a question can be seen as a proper introduction to a story.
Again, the opening question has an informal 'then' tag:

so what did I do this morning then.

This extract again shows how several stories may occur within one Story
element (see superscripts 1, 2 and 3 in the extract). As in Example (23), these
stories are all closely related, but they can be seen as separate entities, each
having a slightly different topical focus. They are, however, in this particular
case, closely related enough actually to overlap, because they all fall into the
general topical category of 'painting and decorating'. The overlaps occur
when one speaker (K) introduces a new (though related) topic, and speaker

C's response is still focused on the previous topic—a tactic referred to by Crow (1983: 142) as 'topic shading'. This happens twice:

1. Topic 1 is in progress:
   C: crazy
   K: I couldn't help but laugh [2] I mean you know *me decorate*
   C: [1] *well you* think it's your eyes don't you
   K: [2] you know me decorate (etc.)
2. Topic 1 is again in progress:
   C: that's ridiculous
   K: yeh . [3] so I just said to *(inaud.)*
   C: [1] *must* have been a whole batch
   K: [3] I said I bought this (etc.)

N.B. This second occurrence in part illustrates how closely related the topics for the stories in this Story are. C's utterance:

> must have been a whole batch

at this point clearly refers back to the first story (1). Later in the extract, however, she makes exactly the same utterance, which is then seen as entirely appropriate for the third story (3):

K: of course you go by what's on the *tin*
C: *nobody* expects them to open each +one+
K: +they+ expect to open ea
C: God
K: but ə
C: must be the whole batch

This whole episode is an excellent example of the dialogic nature of many of the stories in interactions—although the bulk of the information is delivered by K, C takes frequent turns in which she provides firstly EVALUATIONS, e.g. *crazy*, *that's ridiculous*, and secondly additional pieces of information, in the form of guesses, e.g. *must have been a whole batch*.

This example, unlike (22) and (23), does not have an unambiguous ending, such as a summing-up evaluation or a recompletion—instead, there is a minimal *yeh* from the hearer, and an inaudible remark from the teller, with both voices tailing away, so that the story appears really to peter out rather than come to an end.

It is interesting that this example begins with *so*, an item which frequently occurs throughout the data in utterance initial position. When it occurs in this position, as it does here, it indicates a boundary in the conversation—the beginning of a new element—usually Story, and a new topic.

Like the previous examples, the next element in this extract is Speech-in-action, but in this case the speaker who introduces the Speech-in-action does not invite, or allow, any contribution from the hearer. Instead, she uses her Speech-in-action as an introduction to a new story which she wishes to tell.

Example (25) Tape—Celia
          SPEECH-IN-ACTION
Chris: looks better than the last time you saw it
Celia: true yes
(CAT SQUEAKS)
          INTRODUCTION
Celia: hello .
          SPEECH-IN-ACTION
          sorry . didn't mean to ignore you sitting on there -----
          STORY
Chris: she bit Dave yesterday no she didn't she scratched him he said she got
          rabies
Celia: did you see that awful programme
(STORY FOLLOWS ABOUT TV PROGRAMME ABOUT RABIES)
Chris: (inaud.) funnily enough there's a cat with suspected rabies in
          Cumberland now *isn't there*
Celia: *oh God*
          SPEECH-IN-ACTION
Chris: oh look
Celia: I have brung a bottle of wine

Unlike the previous examples, this Story does not open with a question—instead it arises out of the Speech-in-action which precedes it (i.e. the utterance which refers to the cat). The first story which which occurs in this element is completed in the first utterance:

Example (26) Tape—Celia
          she bit Dave yesterday no she didn't she scratched him
                    he said she got rabies

which includes all the components necessary for a story—the participants, the action, the temporal location and the in-built negative evaluation of the item *rabies*. The next speaker picks up the reference to *rabies* to introduce immediately another story about a TV serial about rabies. She does this by using the same tactics as in examples (22), (23) and (24)—asking a question:

          did you see that awful programme.

This shows that a story-opening question is not only used to open a new Story ELEMENT, it can also be used to start a new story WITHIN an existing Story element, as in this case, where the participants move from one story to another without any intervening element, such as Speech-in-action.
    The two speakers in this extract continue collaboratively telling a series of

related stories about the TV programme, even though the stories are not 'news' to either of them—they tell one another about scenes in the programme which they have both watched. There is, however, still a sense in which the telling of these stories is a way of communicating new information— but the new information here is not what HAPPENED, but HOW THE SPEAKER FELT about what happened. The 'new' information here, then, is the personal EVALUATIONS the speakers have made. Nevertheless, the speakers give full dramatic weight to the telling of the action in the stories (even though that action is already known to the hearer); on two occasions, a speaker moves from the conventional simple past tense to the narrative present:

. . . the first one . . . where you SAW him stroking the fox and then you SEE him go in and . . . and you KEPT getting [krε] and then you SEE him cut the lemon . . .

showing that the fact that a hearer already knows a story is not sufficient reason not to tell it.

This example shows the element ending with a final story about a cat in Cumberland, thus taking the speakers out of the area of fictional happenings, back into reality. This final story is preceded by an inaudible remark, which, as the previous examples show, typically occurs when the end of a Story element is in sight for a speaker.

It may be tempting to classify this pair of utterances about the cat in Cumberland as Speech-in-action, rather than Story—it is, after all, a reference to a current event. It does not, however, satisfy the conditions necessary for Speech-in-action, because the speakers themselves are not involved in the action in any way. Whereas most Stories are distinguishable from Speech-in-action by temporal distance from the current encounter, in this case, the action of the Story is distinguishable from Speech-in-action by locational distance—it is completely outside the current encounter (in Cumberland, in fact), and so cannot be, for the participants of the encounter, Speech-in-action.

The participants end this part of their story telling by moving straight on to Speech-in-action, which, again, is concerned with the offer of a gift.

The preceding examples, which are all drawn from my own corpus are in no way idiosyncratic—the London–Lund Corpus contains many examples which display the same characteristics:

Example (27) London–Lund Corpus. Tape—S.2.10
   SPEECH-IN-ACTION
A: my God I'm surrounded with people who +bluff their way through music+
B: +why darling why don't you+ bribe Jo to lend you her Cold Comfort Farm - you've never read it have you -
A: no but I haven't had a baby either

d: *(--- laughs)*
B: *oh honestly
   STORY
   [1] it saved my life in hospital it really did* -
A: actually every every *evening I used to*
d: [2] *it's all right* Arthur **it's it wasn't Jo's she borrowed** it
B: [1] **I couldn't believe it**
d: (. + - + laughs)
   SPEECH-IN-ACTION
c: +hasn't got it anyway+
   STORY
A: [1] +I used to - + I . *I used to go in*
   SPEECH-IN-ACTION
B: *haven't you got it*
c: **no
   STORY
   [2] she borrowed it**
A: [1] **and find . ** Deb *was absolute [diza:]*
B: *[2] my God she wrote* Jo Farmer in it
d: it was my copy .
c: oh I thought it was Ann's or something +ə:m Lyn's+
B: +no no no+ you wrote Jo Farmer *inside* it
d: *no*
   SPEECH-IN-ACTION
c: oh I beg your pardon . oh . sorry . (. coughs)
B: have you got it . Bluff Your Way through Music
d: found your copy
c: Bluff Your Way through Music *- . no I haven't*
   STORY
A: [1] *anyway I used to go into the hospital* in the evenings and find her -- sort
   of in real great pain because she'd laughed so much +she'd burnt a
   couple+ burst a couple of stitches -. [3] except that's the other thing about
   How to Bluff [we] Your Way through Music it's the sort of book that
   people hide -. it was
d: +(-- laughs)+
c: *no (2 sylls.) - goodness no*
B: *no . no*
A: *it was . carefully into the bit of . * place in the bookshelf +where nobody
   would find+
B: +well I didn't find+ it I don't know why you found it [1,2,3] I mean it it's very
   funny and much respected
A: *so I see I'd obviously had no idea*
d: *(---laughs)*

SPEECH-IN-ACTION

B: look three of us here think it's an absolute riot .

A: well I'll **read it then**

B: **you are ** the only philistine amongst us my sweet but never mind you won't (2 to 3 sylls.) [main] me - +(. kisses)+

d: +(- laughs)+ *m*

B: *now . what* was I going to do . seize a cigarlette -

This example is rather more difficult to follow than the previous extracts, because, as often happens in conversations where there are more than two participants, there is a certain amount of overlapping of stories due to competition for the conversational floor. All the stories (see superscripts 1,2,3 and 4) within the sections of Story are closely related, being concerned in some way with the book called *Bluff Your Way Through Music*, but there is considerable competition between the speakers as to which story will be told—A and B repeatedly attempt to tell story [1], while c and d overlap with story [2]. All speakers are, however, collaborating closely to focus on the same general topic of conversation, and, near the end of the extract, speaker B delivers two evaluations:

> I mean it it's very funny and much respected

and, moving into Speech-in-action:

> look three of us here think it's an absolute riot

which actually links stories 1, 2 and 3, and makes clear their relevance to the current situation, i.e. speakers B, c and d have as their goal the persuasion of Speaker A to read the book in question.

The London–Lund Corpus contains many such examples of Story, where the speakers move between the Speech-in-action of the current situation and Story, which provides a topic in which all speakers can join and exchange turns at talking, pieces of information which are part of a particular story, and evaluations, which can be matched so as to further the overall interactional goal of the encounter. Occasionally, a particular speaker will overtly refer to a particular part of the discourse as a story, as in:

Example (28) London–Lund Corpus. Tape—S.1.13

a: you were telling us a . a long complicated story about Eileen's sons last night—I hadn't quite got them in order

B: well she has four boys

a: yes that I think you told me -- *I*

B: *and* none of them have been what you might call ə - very successful in this world -- .

a: *what*

C: *there's* Don . Luke -

a: +(2 sylls.)+
B: +Ben+ Don Luke and Colin
C: Ben Don Luke and Colin ---
B: I think əI find it rather difficult to assess you see . ə(?) in a way Eileen has
    moved into a very sort of—rather outback kind of place - and as a result
    she doesn't əm --- expect perhaps the ə -- the kind of -- successes I suppose
    that -- I mean when we lived in the potteries in our youth—even to know
    (?) anybody who wrote a book was quite something . wasn't it
a: agreed
    (ETC.)

This is a particularly long sequence (see Svartvik and Quirk 1980: 329–40), in
which the speakers move from one story to another while within the general
topical field of *Eileen's sons*, and remain, throughout in Story. Throughout the
whole sequence, the speakers collaborate to exchange stories and pieces of
information, and evaluations are closely and positively matched, as in the
short extract above:

B: (...)was quite something . wasn't it
a: agreed

and, later in the sequence:

C: the general standard of living has gone up hasn't it
a: enormously

This particular sequence ends in a slightly unusual way, similar, in fact, to its
beginning, with an overt reference to the part of the discourse just completed:

Example (29) London-Lund Corpus. Tape—S.1.13
    SPEECH-IN-ACTION
a: well that's Eileen's four . and we covered Margaret - what's her son doing
    now - Dan
C: *Dan -
a: Dan*
    STORY
B: *oh well Dan's doing quite* well he was offered a very good job
    (ETC.)

Speaker a's first utterance in this extract can be properly viewed as Speech-in-
action, because it steps outside Story and refers to the fact that the speakers in
the current encounter have been involved in a particular section of the
discourse which has been classified as Story; the utterance makes explicit
reference, in fact, to the ongoing 'activity' of the current encounter, that
activity being CHATTING.
    The speakers quickly move into yet another Story, prompted again by
Speaker a, who provides a story slot with the question:

what's her son doing now - Dan,

which is then filled by Speaker B, who launches into a new Story.

4.2.3.1 *Conclusions about Story*

As examples (22), (23), (24), (25) and (29) show, questions are frequently used
to introduce stories, both at the beginning of a Story element, and at the
commencement of a new story when the element is already in progress; the
questions used to open the stories, and the results of those questions are:

(22)	did you get lost then	(Story, next speaker)
(23)	did you get a Xmas card	(Story, same speaker)
(24)	so what did I do	(Story, same speaker)
(25)	did you see that	(Story, both speakers)
(29)	what's her son doing now	(Story, next speaker)

Such questions can be seen as opening the way for stories to be told and,
furthermore, that the use of such questions by a speaker is a tactic to ENSURE
that a story will be told. This does not mean, of course, that the following story
will necessarily be told by the NEXT speaker—the question may well be a tactic
to allow the SAME speaker to tell the story, even in cases where the second
speaker provides an answer to the question. The framing of a question in
order to produce an answer which can be FOLLOWED by a story appears to be a
way of signalling that the dialogue is still in progress, while ensuring that the
conversational turn must return to the questioner, who then becomes the
story teller; As Schegloff says (Laver and Hutcheson 1972: 385): 'It seems to
be a property of many QA [question and answer] sequences that the asker of a
question has the RIGHT to talk again.'

There is also an optional element in the taking up of these story tellings,
which is illustrated in Example (25), where BOTH speakers CHOOSE to
collaborate in telling the story. This option is always present in such cases, so
a hearer always has the option to join in the story-telling, perhaps by GUESSING
parts of the story, even when the facts are unknown to him/her.

These comments on the tactical nature of the questions in the examples do
not imply that ALL questions have similar powers. In dialogue, there are often
questions which do not produce, and are not designed to produce, stories as a
result. One example would be the kind of question which arises in Speech-in-
action, such as:

would you like a glass of wine.

There are also a number of questions in the data which closely resemble the
story openers, but which, again, do not have the same function, such as:

> which one d'you get it on and
> haven't you got the straps.

These do not OPEN stories, but they occur WITHIN a story, and are designed to elicit more details of that story. The story-opening questions can be distinguished from other kinds of question by the combination of two factors:

1. the introduction of a new conversational topic; this distinguishes them from the questions which arise WITHIN an existing story.
2. use of the simple past tense; this distinguishes them from the questions which arise in Speech-in-action.

Another point, associated with these observations on the function of questions, which is illustrated in the above examples, is that story-telling in conversation is very much a collaborative exercise. The most extreme example of this is Example (25), where both speakers take turns to tell part of the story, but even the other examples show that, when a story is being told by one speaker, there are frequent contributions from the other speaker.

The one exception to this is the very short story which is shown as Example (26). This is the only one which is told completely by a single contribution from one speaker:

> she bit Dave yesterday no she didn't she scratched him
> he said she got rabies.

This is unlike all the other examples, in that there is not even an evaluation, or a token turn ('mm') from the hearer.

4.2.4 Closings

This highly ritualised element is difficult to exemplify, due to one of the main problems associated with surreptitious tape recording; tape cassettes can only cope with forty-five minutes of recording before they stop, and to continue recording the cassette must be turned over. When the recording is surreptitious, this is, of course, impossible, with the result that it is extremely difficult to obtain tape recordings of closings of interactions, most interactive encounters being longer than forty-five minutes. This practical difficulty accounts for the lack of Closings in the tapes which provide my own examples, and it is, presumably, similar difficulties which account for a similar lack in the interactive encounters which form part of the London–Lund Corpus. I do, however, have one example of a face-to-face Closing, which is transcribed, not from tape, but from memory. This was written down immediately after it occurred; the reader will be familiar with many similar examples:

Example (30)
P: I must go - taking up your time - have a nice day tomorrow

C: oh thanks and thanks again for the things - this is lovely - cyclamen isn't it - cyclamen
P: yeh . cyclamen . I think it is
C: 's gorgeous - have a lovely time
P: all this evening to look forward to . ooh (squeak)
C: enjoy it
P: I will
C: have a lovely time and thanks again
P: thanks . bye
C: bye
P: bye

This example illustrates the highly repetitive nature of Closings, with speakers repeating items from their own, and one another's utterances. The tactic used to initiate the Closing is one of those described by Laver (1975: 230)—an expression of concern for the HEARER, which is presented as the reason for initiating the Closing:

I must go - taking up your time.

The speakers then go on with the Closing, meshing repetitive well-wishings for their future activities with expressions of thanks, both for a gift which has changed hands (a cyclamen), and also for the well-wishings themselves:

C: have a lovely time and thanks again
P: thanks

Between the fourth and eighth utterances there is, in this sequence, a delay in the progress of the Closing, a frequent occurrence in Closings, and referred to in some detail by Schegloff and Sacks (in Turner 1974: 233–64). What the speakers do here is (to follow Schegloff and Sacks's terminology) to 'open up a closing'. The *have a lovely time* in utterance 4, is clearly a reference back to a topic which has already been discussed earlier in the conversation, such a reference being typical of closing sequences. The speaker of utterance 5 reopens (in a small way) this topic with:

all this evening to look forward to . ooh (squeak),

thus obliging the other speaker to continue with the topic for at least one more utterance:

enjoy it,

and the 'reopening' speaker then provides a further contribution to the same re-opened topic with:

I will.

At this point, the next speaker makes a second attempt to proceed with the Closing by repeating the part of utterance 4 which led to the reopening of the topic, and following this immediately with a further token which is typical of Closings:

thanks again,

the *again* serving to underline that this is part of a CLOSING sequence. This signal of wishing to proceed with the Closing is this time taken up by the other speaker, who also delivers a *thanks* and accompanies this, after a short pause, with *bye*, which takes the sequence to the final tokens of Closing. Two more *bye*s are exchanged, and the encounter is finished.

Although this example of a face-to-face Closing is alone in the interactive data, it does, as the above analysis shows, exhibit many of the characteristics of 'closings' (Schegloff and Sacks) or 'parting phases' (Laver), and can, therefore, be taken as typical.

Examples of Closings in telephone interactions are more readily available, and Jefferson's corpus contains several, of which the following is typical:

Example (31) Jefferson's tape—NB:II:3:R
Emma: .hhhhhhh OKAY HONEY WELL AH'LL TAHLK WIH YIH
       *NEX'WEEK *
Lottie: *u -:-:-:*
Emma: +MAYBE AH'LL STAY DOWN AH'LL SEE+
Lottie: +uh+ O*kay honey*
Emma: *eh* AA'R+IGHT+
Lottie: +Right+
Emma: B*ye*
Lottie: *Bye b*ye

This example resembles Example (30) in that speakers repeat tokens from one another's utterances as they proceed towards termination of the interaction, but this example contains no temporary reopening or reinvoking of a topic during the actual Closing.

4.3 Conclusions

The preceding exemplification has shown that there are certain elements which appear to dominate interaction to such an extent that they could be described as obligatory; these elements are Speech-in-action and Story.

Contrary to expectations, Introduction is not an obligatory element, although it would be reasonable to suppose that it would be, together with Closing. Inspection of the data shows, however, that this assumption is incorrect in that an introductory phase is not always present, and that, when it is absent, the participants behave as though this is a perfectly normal occurrence, so that the introductory phase, while often occurring at the beginning of interactions, is not an obligatory element. The closing phase, however, does appear to be obligatory, although, as already explained, there are practical difficulties in demonstrating this.

The elements identified in the preceding sections do not simply occur in a purely haphazard fashion throughout interaction. There is a certain loose ordering of elements—not so inflexible that each element has its pre-determined place in any given interaction, but, as will be evident from observation of the data referred to, there is a high degree of predictability about the occurrence of Speech-in-action at, or near, the beginning of an encounter, and an equally high degree of predictability that the vast bulk of an interaction will consist of story-tellings.

From the analysis of the interactive data several observations can be made:

1. In general, topics in dialogue are progressed by means of Story.
2. Speech-in-action is potentially an opening for Story, and may range over a variety of different topics until one becomes an opening for a story. The stories which follow may then be accounts of stories in the past, or they may be plans for the more distant future.
3. Both speakers may co-operate (using the turn-taking system) to turn Speech-in-action into Story.
4. One speaker may begin with Speech-in-action and immediately progress to Story in the same utterance.
5. Story is the element which takes up the greatest part of speakers' time in casual conversation, Speech-in-action appearing to serve primarily to LINK Stories.
6. A story is not necessarily 'news'—it may be known to speaker AND hearer, and still be told, and heard, as a story. When this is the case, the story may be told co-operatively, with both speakers using their conversational 'turns' to make substantial contributions.
7. When a story IS 'news' to the hearer, this does not guarantee that the 'teller' will tell the story alone. A hearer who does not know the facts of the story will frequently take more than minimal, encouraging turns, and attempt to provide pieces of the story by guessing.

An interesting point has emerged from a close inspection of discoursal stories: although they occur within encounters which have an overall interactional goal, they are (internally) concerned with transactional sequences—all the above examples involve descriptions of past transactions.

All these observations show that interactive discourse is constructed through the use of forms of spoken communication within which speakers can co-operatively represent themselves as involved in joint activity—either in the area of Speech-in-action, or in Story.

4.4 Stories, Speech-in-action and Status

If one considers the overall goal of interactional encounters—i.e. the development of the relationship between the speakers—which, as I have explained in Chapter 2, section 2.2, is dependent on the negotiation of the relative status of the speech participants, the reason for the predominance of stories in such encounters becomes clear.

The structure of dialogic stories is such as to allow both speakers to take turns at providing topics and sub-topics, asking for and providing details, and giving evaluations. In other words, the collaborative telling of stories permits both speakers to take control of the dialogue at different times, while, in pursuing the story, preserving the potential for the NEXT speaker to take control in his/her turn. As control is clearly the province of the SUPERIOR speaker, stories function to allow the EXCHANGE of superior status throughout the dialogue.

As the preceding discussion and exemplification has shown, when stories cannot be strung together by some kind of topic fitment, speakers move into Speech-in-action for a short period. This can be viewed, in status terms, as a return to base—a 'break' in the conversation—during which the main flow of the dialogue, with its continual exchange of superior status, is interrupted. During such a period, there may well be remarks which are 'other-oriented'— thus signalling the adoption of some degree of superior status on the part of the speaker—but, as the stretches of Speech-in-action tend, in general, to be very short when compared with stretches of Story, they do not allow sufficient time for the development of any extended status imbalance, and do not, therefore, occasion any repair. The impact they have on the quality of the interaction is, therefore, negligible, and I suggest, therefore, that they approach very closely the supposedly 'opening' category, suggested by Laver, of 'neutral tokens'.

The major 'bulk' of interaction takes place through the medium of Story, and it appears that, apart from the undoubted benefit of allowing speakers to exchange roles, Story has the advantage (throughout whatever sequence of stories it incorporates) of allowing (and, indeed, requiring) evaluations to be exchanged and matched at frequent intervals, thereby providing linguistic evidence of solidarity produced by the verbal interaction of the speakers.

It is worth noting that the stories which are told throughout interactional encounters are, in fact, presented by the speakers as accounts of TRANS-ACTIONS. It appears, then, that, when speakers meet for the primary purpose of interacting, their main method of doing this is by reference to previous transactional encounters; extended interaction can thus be seen as a kind of 'transaction at one remove'.

5 Repairs in interactional dialogue

Chapters 3 and 4 show the components of the interactive basis of dialogue and the predictability of their occurrence throughout various kinds of conversation. The ways in which speech participants use, or dispense with, the various elements, and the ways in which these elements tend to be linked are discussed in the context of job interviews, a tutorial and several examples of informal chat. The examples used show the flow of conversation, with each element leading smoothly on, with the consent of both (or all) participants, into each next element.

There are, however, occasions when, for some reason, the flow is not so smooth, and the course of the conversation is temporarily interrupted or even permanently diverted. It is just these occasions which I propose to deal with now, as they provide the most precise evidence for predictability in conversation. Whereas the preceding discussion has illustrated the predictability of KINDS of talk (Speech-in-action, Story, etc.) in the various forms of conversation, the evidence which I shall present in this chapter will go further than this, and will illustrate a strong predictability of DIRECTION in conversation. This is not to claim that it is possible, given the transcription of any conversation, to predict exactly WHAT will be said next, but, as my examples will show, there are frequent occurrences in conversation which, once detected, allow the analyst to predict confidently WHERE the conversation will go next. These occurrences are DISRUPTIONS in the ongoing interaction, and the directional consequences to which they give rise are in the nature of what I refer to as 'Scapegoats' and 'Topic Loops', both of which will be described and exemplified in the succeeding paragraphs.

Disruption in an ongoing conversation can be either (a) PRACTICAL, or (b) INTERACTIONAL. The following sections will explain the difference between practical and interactional disruption, will show what sort of items cause disruption, and how speakers deal with the disruption when it does arise. Because disruption, whether practical or interactional, results in 'extra' conversational work for the speakers, I shall refer to disruption of whatever kind as 'trouble', and the work done as a result of it as 'repair'.

5.1 Practical trouble

I have referred, in the preceding section, to 'practical' trouble, and this requires some further explanation. The practical aspect of the conversational encounter is the area which is concerned with the ability of speakers to understand one another's utterances at the basic level of hearing correctly, ensuring that they send verbal messages which accord with their intentions, and ensuring that they have correctly received the verbal messages from their co-conversationalist.

5.1.1 Practical troubles and their repairs

In ethnomethodological studies of conversation, a considerable amount of work has been done on topic management, and one aspect of this which has been developed by Jefferson, is the area of 'side sequences', which occur DURING discussion of a 'main' topic. In Sudnow 1972 (294–338), Jefferson describes in some detail the kind of 'side sequences' which arise in conversation in order to effect a repair to the current topic.

A brief description of the various repairs she discusses will show that these are PRACTICAL repairs, occasioned by PRACTICAL troubles.

The types listed and exemplified by Jefferson are:

1. Repeat, Laugh token (sometimes alternated with syllables of a repeated item), Interrogative, Misapprehension: all of which call into question a particular item from the preceding utterance, and ask for this item to be corrected (if the 'wrong' item has been used), or demand clarification of the item or some aspect of the item. The initiation of such a repair is a COMPETITIVE action, which provides some kind of challenge to the preceding speaker.
2. Affirmation: which provides a piece of 'side' information, which the current speaker either does not know or has forgotten, and which is necessary to the successful continuation of the ongoing turn. This kind of repair is, of course, non-competitive, in that it is designed to HELP the current speaker continue with his/her topic and his/her conversational turn.
3. Expanded action: which enables the initiator to 'pass' his/her turn on to another speaker, on the grounds that that other speaker is a more appropriate person to take the turn. This kind of repair is neither competitive nor helpful—it serves simply to allow a speaker to opt out of a

particular sequence in the conversation, while allowing the sequence itself to proceed.

As the brief descriptions above show, these are, indeed, all practical repairs, concerned with the actual turn-by-turn progress of the conversation, and the clarification of troublesome items which, if unrepaired, could lead to misunderstandings which would impede that progress. They all initiate side sequences, which, once complete, ensure that the speakers will return to the mainstream of the conversation.

5.2 A wider view of repairs

I do not intend to argue with the above analysis of repairs—it is clear that such repairs do frequently occur in interactional data. I do, however, take the view that this kind of analysis, which concentrates on the PRACTICAL aspect, reveals only PART of the system of conversational repairs, because it fails to appreciate the full significance of a repair in terms of the overall purpose of the encounter—the development of the interpersonal relationship between the speakers. In other words, Jefferson's approach makes clear the practical operations involved in repairs, but neglects the role of repairs in terms of the INTERACTION of the participants. The following sections of this chapter will deal with this neglected interactional aspect, and will also show that an analysis from this point of view adds further to an understanding of the practical workings of the whole encounter, particularly in the area of topic movement, as it will be shown, throughout all the following examples, that one of the consequences of a repair is the collaborative production of what I call a TOPIC LOOP, where a topic from earlier in the conversation is reinvoked either in order to provide an escape from a troublesome area of the discourse, or in order to 'rerun' a previously troublesome topic uncontroversially.
N.B. My use of the term 'Topic' is not intended to mean SENTENTIAL topic (as opposed to sentential 'comment'), it is, rather, intended to mean CONVERSA-TIONAL topic (i.e. what is being talked about).

5.3 Interactional trouble

Interactional trouble does not arise only at the level of practical communication—it is not simply a matter of matching the verbal message sent by the speaker with that received by the hearer. It is trouble which arises in the RELATIONSHIP of the co-conversationalists; this kind of trouble always arises from some alteration in the current interactional balance of the encounter—it is a change in the status differential between the speakers, which, if prolonged, becomes problematic for them.

5.3.1 Interactional troubles and their repairs

These troubles, unlike the practical ones discussed above, are not in any sense subsidiary to the topic from which they arise, and they are not simply resolved by a short side sequence, where, in a few short utterances, a repair can be effected, so that speakers can quickly revert to the mainstream of the conversation. Instead, they tend to be the occasion of large amounts of repair work by speakers, leading to substantial topic movements in conversation. They do, however, sometimes have close connections with practical repairs, in that speakers can manipulate the initiation of practical repairs to such an extent that interactional trouble ensues and an interactional repair becomes necessary. The following sections will illustrate the workings involved.

5.3.2 Status as a source of interactional trouble

Problems arising from status differentials can cause interactional trouble, but it should be noted that, when interactional trouble does arise, it does not always occasion repair work by the speakers; whether or not repair work is necessary depends on the original status balance of the encounter. To make this point clear it is necessary to consider the different kinds of status balance which may exist in encounters.

A conversational encounter may take place between equal or non-equal participants. Alongside this feature of equality (or non-equality) there is also, of course, the transactional or interactional nature of the encounter and (yet another dimension) the degree of formality. There are certain combinations of these three aspects which operate to remove the possibility of interactional trouble from the encounter, and other combinations which do not operate to remove the possibility of interactional trouble, but which do remove the necessity for a repair, and in which the speakers have access to other ways of getting round the trouble. The following table, with its examples, shows how the various aspects may combine to characterise particular types of conversational encounter:

1. Equal + Informal + Interactional—(a chat between friends)
2. Equal + Informal + Transactional—(friends planning to meet for lunch)
3. Equal + Formal + Transactional—(civil court action)
4. Equal + Formal + Interactional—(TV chat show)
5. Non-equal + Informal + Interactional—(teacher chatting to pupil)
6. Non-equal + Formal + Interactional—(visiting dignitary chatting with workers)
7. Non-equal + Formal + Transactional—(job interview)
8. Non-equal + Informal + Transactional—(parent and child discussing pocket money)

As can be seen from the examples used in the table above, the classifications of 'formal' and 'informal' are taken to indicate the extent to which the participants know beforehand what will happen during the encounter. It is, of course, the case that, in certain interactions between intimates, participants may know beforehand what will happen, but this kind of foreknowledge rests on the past experience of the individual, together with detailed knowledge of the personality and background of the co-conversationalist; it is an IDIO-SYNCRATIC foreknowledge. The kind of foreknowledge which is associated with the formality of the encounter can be seen as an INSTITUTIONALISED foreknowledge, as it arises, not out of facts learned about a private individual, but out of facts learned about the workings of society and its institutions, facts which are known to society in general.

It should be noted here that the examples I have provided for different kinds of conversational encounter illustrate only a few of the possible variations in status/formality configurations; status and formality are concepts which embrace a wide variety of fine distinctions, and there are examples which could be found where the comments in the following sections would have to be modified in order to take such distinctions into account.

There would, for example, be a difference between the management of interactional trouble in a job interview (where the inferior participant—the interviewee—expects, and is granted, comparatively high status) and in a parole board interview (where the inferior participant—the prisoner—expects, and is granted, only very low status). The descriptions I have used, and the examples which illustrate them, are designed to differentiate between conversational encounters in a general way, and to provide some general guide lines to understanding some of the considerations apparently employed by speech participants in their choice of tactics for dealing with interactional trouble.

5.3.3 Where interactional trouble can arise

Among the eight different types of conversational encounter listed in 5.3.2 above, there are two which are so formally structured as to disallow the occurrence of interactional trouble. These are:

No. 3. (Equal + Formal + Transactional, e.g. a civil court action), where proceedings are controlled and monitored by officials who have complete authority over the management of the encounter. No status imbalance is allowed to occur, so no interactional trouble can arise.

No. 6. (Non-equal + Formal + Interactional, e.g. a visiting dignitary chatting to workers), where, again, proceedings are highly controlled by officials whose special task is to ensure the smooth and trouble-free running of the encounter.

Of the remaining six types, there are three categories of conversational encounter where interactional trouble may arise, and where, if this trouble does arise, a repair is necessary:

No. 1. (Equal + Informal + Interactional—a chat between friends),
No. 2. (Equal + Informal + Transactional—friends planning to meet for lunch), and
No. 4. (Equal + Formal + Interactional—a TV chat show).

Of these three types, Nos. 1 and 2 can be regarded as sufficiently similar to allow for comments on one type to apply also to the other type, because both are informal and between equals. Such conversational encounters can, and often do, incorporate both transactional and interactional material, so that, for example, a casual chat between friends may well become transactional in the area of a particular topic or topics, and, in the same way, an informal transaction between equals may well, if the participants begin to exchange chat in a friendly way apart from, or in addition to, the transaction in progress, become primarily an interaction. The data at my disposal are largely 'coffee cup chat'—so an analysis of this will suffice to give exemplification of trouble and repairs in both these categories.

The same can be said of No. 4 (TV chat show), as the formality of this kind of encounter lies in the restrictions put upon the encounter by the timetabling of television programmes, the need for orientation in favour of good camera shots, and the like; the actual encounter itself is likely to be (and is, indeed, designed to be) similar to a private, casual chat between friends. The 'coffee cup chats' used for exemplification here will, then, be sufficient to cover this category too.

There are two further types of conversational encounter which fall into the category which do not preclude the occurrence of interactional trouble, but which do not necessitate a following repair. These are:

No. 5. (Non-equal + Informal + Interactional, e.g. a teacher chatting to a pupil), and
No. 8. (Non-equal + Informal + Transactional, e.g. a parent and child discussing the payment of pocket money).

In both these cases, interactional trouble may arise, with the inferior participant taking on a role more suited to the superior participant by, perhaps, broaching disallowed topics (asking the teacher how much he/she earns), or using disallowed grammatical forms such as imperatives (*give me five pounds a week*). If this does happen, however, the basic (non-situationally bound) status differential between the participants provides for a CORRECTION to restore the balance of superior/inferior. In both cases, the superior has the RIGHT to 'pull rank' on the inferior, to comment overtly on the attempt to seize undue status (usually by a negative evaluation: *I don't like your attitude*, or a negative imperative: *Don't talk to me like that*, or *Don't be cheeky*).

Wilson (unpublished Ph.D. thesis) discusses in some detail what I have here called 'corrections'—where an acknowledged superior (parent or teacher) reinvokes the latent status differential between the speakers; Wilson's term for this phenomenon is 'institutionalised out-moding', the status differential in such encounters having its roots in an institution of the society (e.g. the family, or the schooling system). Part of his argument is that 'institutionalised non-equals' are able to (and do frequently) relinquish their non-equality in order to interact as equals during what I have referred to as a 'chat', or what he refers to as a 'conversation'. He claims that, while in 'conversational mode', the rights and duties of such speakers are in all ways equal, and that a chat between such participants is, therefore, directly equivalent to a chat between 'true' equals (e.g. intimate friends).

Wilson's recognition (and thorough exemplification) of the institutionalised out-mode provides, however, evidence that the rights of institutionalised non-equals are not, in the final analysis, equal, even during a chat, because, whatever appearance of equality may be assumed for the encounter, the superior participant ALWAYS has access to the institutionalised out-mode, whereas the inferior participant NEVER does. It is this access, open to the superior speaker, which means that when interactional trouble does arise in an encounter of this kind, it can be (and is) dealt with by a CORRECTION, which obviates the need for a repair.

5.3.4 Causes of trouble and resulting repair work

I have indicated, in section 5.3 above, that interactional trouble stems from a change in the status balance of the encounter, which is caused by one participant adopting the role of superior, and the other participant adopting (or being forced to adopt) the complementary role of inferior. This is a troublesome matter in an encounter between equals where there is no rigidly formal structure to control the interaction, because it changes one of the basic characteristics of the encounter—the equality of the speakers. This equality is, it should be noted, not necessarily in the area of social or financial standing, intelligence, or any other aspect of the participants' lives OUTSIDE the encounter; it is SPEAKER equality WITHIN the encounter, and relates, therefore, to equal rights to speak, to select topics, to ask questions, to withhold information—in general, equal rights to take turns at adopting the superior role. (As my remarks in the previous section have indicated, there are certain roles and status patternings in society which do not allow true speaker equality even within the encounter, as in the case of the parent and child involved in a TRANSACTIONAL encounter about pocket money or the like.) The preservation of those rights for each speaker in an equal encounter of this kind is the preservation of what Goffman (1955,) calls 'face', and, as Goffman says: 'maintenance of face is a condition of interaction'. Loss of 'face' is, then, a severe disruption in interaction—it is, indeed, 'trouble' for the interactants, and interaction must be 'repaired', so that 'face' can be restored. Goffman discusses the ways in which this can be achieved, and describes a series of steps which speech participants take to deal with the trouble.

After the initial 'offence' occurs, there is first the 'challenge', where participants acknowledge that trouble has arisen. Next comes the 'offering', where the offender is given a chance to make good the offence; this may be done by declaring the troublesome remark(s) to be a joke, or a mistake. If the offender does not use this strategy, he/she can (if it is another speaker's face which he has threatened, rather than his own) offer 'compensation' to the injured party (in the form, perhaps, of an apology), and/or he can display 'self-punishment' (by overtly criticising his own actions in causing the offence).

N.B. The maintenance of 'face' is, of course, not only a phenomenon of equal encounters—suitable and appropriate 'face' must be maintained by all participants in all encounters, and must be related to the amount of status due to the incumbent of each role. However, as the subsequent discussion will show, my arguments and claims about interactional repairs focus primarily on the preservation of 'face' in equal, interactional encounters, as it is in such encounters that the most painstaking and meticulous work must be done in order to maintain 'face' and preserve the interactional balance between the speakers.

The steps described by Goffman which speakers use to effect a repair relate to the kind of trouble which is, presumably, overtly linguistically recognised by the participants. Not all interactional trouble falls into this category—the kinds of trouble which arise in the data on which this work is based can be seen as COVERTLY acknowledged trouble. Its repair is necessary to PREVENT overt acknowledgement that trouble has arisen; it is this kind of trouble and its consequent repair work, involving a special kind of interactional strategy which I call a SCAPEGOAT REPAIR, which will be exemplified and discussed in the following sections.

5.3.5 Covertly acknowledged trouble and Scapegoat Repairs

Covertly acknowledged trouble can arise in several ways, all of them connected with an imbalance in the established status pattern of the encounter. I propose to discuss three major types which the reader will intuitively recognise as commonly occurring in interactional encounters. I shall refer to them as:

(1) Depersonification

(2) Alienation by imperative
(3) Evaluation conflict.

The following sections will show how these troubles arise in dialogue, and how, when they do arise, speakers can perform special repairs, using a particular kind of status patterning involving a SCAPEGOAT.

5.3.5.1 *Depersonification*

Example (1) Tape—Dawsons
(GEOFF, JACK, CHRIS AND CATHERINE (ALL ADULTS) HAVE BEEN TALKING FOR SOME TIME, WHEN MARY (A CHILD) ENTERS THE ROOM)

	INTRODUCTION
Geoff:	I'm Geoff *hallo*
Chris:	*(laugh)*
Jack:	this is Mary
Geoff:	*hallo Mary*
	SPEECH-IN-ACTION
Jack:	*SHE's ten and* +SHE's very big+
	INTRODUCTION
Mary:	+hallo+
	SPEECH-IN-ACTION
Jack:	*and SHE's got long hair*
Chris:	*(laugh)*
Geoff:	SHE's very pretty
	STORY
Jack:	y . ahhh . that's I always say that to HER . and SHE k hits me when . *SHE hits me when I (inaud.)*
Others:	*(laugh)*
	INTRODUCTION
Jack:	this is Chris - +(inaud.)+
Mary:	+hallo+
Chris:	hallo
Jack:	(inaud.) one of my customers so you've got to be very polite to him
Geoff:	Chris is (inaud.) as well
Chris:	(laugh)
Jack:	(inaud.) one of my customers too - oh (inaud.)
	SPEECH-IN-ACTION
	Mary's good at selling
Geoff:	*(laugh)*
Chris:	*(laugh)*

This example involves two speakers, Jack and Geoff, talking about another speaker, Mary, as though she is not present—as though she is, in fact, an object to be discussed, rather than a conversational participant (the utterances used for Introduction are, in fact, interleaved with Speech-in-action). This particular kind of interactional trouble must frequently arise when adults and children mix. What the two 'offenders' are doing by this is not simply creating (or underlining) an inferior role for the child, by referring to her as though she is not present—they are, in fact, depriving her of ALL status in the encounter, so that she is, in effect, DEPERSONIFIED in the context of the ongoing interaction.

The linguistic manifestation of this trouble is the unusually high incidence of the third-person singular pronoun, bearing in mind that the person thus referred to is present. Between them, Geoff and Jack use a pronoun to refer to Mary seven times in this extract (see *emphasis), without, in that particular section, using her name once. This is typical of talk about a third person who is NOT present in the encounter.

The status balance of the encounter (which has hitherto rested on the equality of all participants) has, therefore, been disrupted, and the speech participants are in a state of interactional trouble.

There is, as I have already mentioned, no overt linguistic acknowledgement of this kind of trouble, and it becomes obvious that the POTENTIAL trouble which can be expected to arise from this kind of talk has become actual trouble for the participants because they immediately begin to perform a repair of it. A transcription of what happens next in the conversation will show that this is indeed a repair, and is occasioned by the preceding troublesome section:

Example (2) Tape—Dawsons

Jack: now what was I gonna say . oh yes . əm .TOM . AND MYRTLE CARTER say that they'll be a little bit *late*

Others: *(laugh)*

Geoff: now that's funny actually +because+

Chris: +(laugh)+

Geoff: I was having a drink with him in the pub you know like one does and *(inaud.)*

Others: *(laugh)*

Geoff: and HE THREW UP ACROSS THE BAR . I mean I'd never've believed it myself but AFTER HE'D SCOOPED IT UP then he said he was gonna make his way home and then he'd be better and +(inaud.) by nine o'clock+

Others: +(inaud.)+

Chris: was it in a pub he bought you a drink *(inaud.) I thought it was (inaud.)*

Jack: *(inaud.)*
Geoff: OUR BELOVED LEADER has bought me a drink this evening . I think
            THAT MEANS I'M GONNA BE SACKED +(inaud., laughing)+
Chris: +(laugh)+
Jack: well that's what ə: JMC . MC . Marsh-Collins says that if the
            director twinkles at you n nicely *like he does*
Geoff: *yeh . VERY BAD +SIGN+
JACK: +VERY DODGY+ cause if he comes *into the . front sales office*
Catherine: *SMILE ON THE FACE OF THE TIGER*
Jack: and əthe sales department that's Joan and Neil and myself
            SPEECH-IN-ACTION
Catherine: +mind Jack mind your mind your mind your . gesticulations+
            STORY
Jack: +are sitting there *in the corner*+
Geoff: *(laugh)*
Chris: *ahh . yes (laugh)*
Jack: +beaming and twinkling and the cheeks go all sort of round and
            red+
Others: +(laugh)+
Jack: and əI think oh that's nice the director's twinkling at us you know
            cause he's sort of you know paternally like that . he stands about
            the place going (noise) (gesture)
Others: (laugh)
Jack: I said to Marsh-Collins one morning cause he gives me lifts I said
            əm the director twinkled at the sales department when we were
            sitting there and he said DANGEROUS *DANGEROUS*
Geoff: *DANGEROUS* SIGN +THAT+
Chris: +yeh+
            SPEECH-IN-ACTION
Jack: I'll do the wiping up and I'll (inaud.)
Others: (inaud.)
Chris: cheers
Geoff: yes . cheers
Catherine: cheers .
Chris: mmm
            INTRODUCTION
Jack: welcome .
            STORY
            what news well did you find your way alright then
            (ETC.)

    At the end of the 'offending' section, Jack mentions Mary by name, rather
than using another pronoun, and it may be that this marks a return of Jack's

recognition of her as a conversational participant, a holder of some status in the encounter. He shows awareness of the trouble which has arisen by this immediate change of topic. The trouble which has arisen is, of course, not only trouble for Mary, who is the inferior participant, it is also trouble for Jack and Geoff, who have shown themselves taking up a superior role towards her, and, as Goffman (1971) says: 'the member of any group . . . is expected to go to certain lengths to save the feelings and the face of others present' (322).

Jack not only changes the topic of conversation, he marks this by the metastatement:

> now what was I gonna say.

He then introduces a mention of two people who are NOT present in the encounter:

> Tom and Myrtle Carter,

one of whom, Tom, becomes the topic for discussion for the following utterances.

As the extract shows, Tom is discussed, primarily by Jack and Geoff (the original offenders) in a series of wholly negative evaluations (see emphasised sections), and it appears that Tom has been introduced as a topic of conversation purely for this purpose. He is, then, a SCAPEGOAT, and his conversational value lies in his ability to be thus used.

It is worth noting that even the first mention of Tom's name, in Jack's first utterance in this section, raises a laugh from the other participants, and it is safe to assume that this is a signal that they all immediately recognise him as a Scapegoat. As the rest of the section makes clear, he is, actually, a most suitable Scapegoat for interactional trouble, because he is (a) known to all participants, particularly the two offenders, Jack and Geoff, and (b) the director of the firm where both Geoff and Jack work. He is, then, a suitable candidate for criticism in any interaction between them, and can be regarded as a kind of 'institutionalised Scapegoat'.

After the introduction of Tom as a potential Scapegoat, the assembled group perform twenty-nine utterances in which the Scapegoat is mocked and criticised, primarily by Jack and Geoff, while other participants provide laughing encouragement.

The purpose of this Scapegoat sequence seems to be to divert the attention of the participants from the offence against a person present (Mary) by directing a series of offences towards a person absent (Tom). In this way, the participants can recover from the status imbalance, where they were on opposite sides of a superior/inferior barrier, WITHOUT ever overtly acknowledging that that imbalance has occurred. The pattern of superior versus inferior is maintained over this sequence, but, instead of it resulting in a loss of face by a participant, it is directed harmlessly outside the encounter to the

Scapegoat, who, not being present, does not suffer any real threat to his face. All the participants are, in fact, acting as superiors, the inferior being the Scapegoat.

The Scapegoat sequence ends with Jack's utterance:

> . . . dangerous dangerous,

which is what Goldberg (in Schenkein 1978: 211) refers to as a 'recompletion', and is typically a topic terminating signal. The second part of this recompletion is overlapped by Geoff, with:

> dangerous sign that,

thus reinforcing Jack's recompletion; and this, in turn, is overlapped by Chris:

> yeh

which brings the repair sequence to an end, use of the Scapegoat having restored equality to the current encounter.

5.3.5.1.1 Topic loop

When the Scapegoat sequence finishes in the extract—with the reinforced recompletion followed by 'yeh'—Jack immediately introduces a new topic, in the form of Speech-in- action:

> I'll do the wiping up and I'll (inaud.),

but the others do not join in with this new topic—instead, they perform a ritualistic well-wishing, associated with drinking alcohol:

> cheers.

Neither of these new topics is adopted as a major topic for conversation—presumably there is not a great deal of mileage in either. For practical purposes, the participants are 'without' a topic of conversation; an offence has been committed, a Scapegoat has been found and has taken criticism to divert attention from the offence, the status balance has been restored, but the speakers are now without anything to talk about. A suitable topic must be provided, and—although this is not essential—a suitable speaker to provide such a topic is one of the offenders; he, in part, causes the trouble, he provides and exploits the Scapegoat, and it is appropriate that he should restore the conversation to 'normal', i.e. provide a Story in which the other speakers can collaborate, or create an opening for another speaker to provide a Story.

There are, of course, constraints on such a speaker; he has only recently extricated himself and his co-conversationalists from trouble which he has caused, and he has provided and exhausted the potential of a Scapegoat. If he is now to provide a new topic for conversation, it MUST be non-controversial, in terms of the encounter, i.e. non-face threatening to any participant. His choice of topic must, then, be extremely careful—it cannot be anything which could be seen as threatening by any participant.

The topic which might most readily spring to mind in such circumstances could, perhaps, be the weather. This is, however, very rarely used in such cases, perhaps because to talk about the weather is to take the conversation OUTSIDE the encounter. What is needed here is to introduce a topic agreeable to all participants, guaranteed (or unlikely) to give offence, and with the capacity to provide extended talk, which can, eventually, provide a lead to different topics.

In this particular example, Jack chooses to create a suitable slot for the visitors (Geoff and Chris) to provide a Story, and he does this by reintroducing a topic which has already been dealt with earlier in the encounter, albeit when he was not present. It is, nevertheless, even in his mention of it, clearly a topic from earlier in the conversation:

welcome . what news well did you find your way alright then.

This is, clearly, a topic more suitable to the opening of the conversation, and it has, in fact, already been run at the opening (see Example (22), Chapter 4, section 4.2.3). Although Jack was not present at this time, it is certain that he is aware of the 'natural' placement for such a topic, and this awareness provides, in a way, a valid reason for his selection of it as a topic for talk now, because it is, in a sense, a 'tried and tested' topic; it has already been run once without troublesome incident, so it is a 'safe' topic for this rather sensitive time after a trouble and its repair. What Jack has performed here is, in fact, a 'Topic Loop', by reverting to a topic which progressed safely and non-controversially at an earlier time in the conversation. This can be seen as reinforcing the wiping out of the trouble and providing a new start for the speech participants.

This is not an isolated instance of such a manoeuvre—co-conversationalists do tend to perform similar manoeuvres in similar circumstances in order to restore harmony to a current encounter which has run into trouble; further exemplification will support this claim.

5.3.5.2 *Alienation by imperative*

Example (3) Tape—Celia
(CELIA BEGINS TO TELL CHRIS ABOUT SOME PROBLEMS SHE HAS HAD WITH DECORATING, THEY COLLABORATE TO ESTABLISH EXACTLY WHAT THE PROBLEM IS, THEN CHRIS BEGINS A VERY LENGTHY ATTACK ON CELIA, WHERE SHE REPEATEDLY GIVES NEGATIVE EVALUATION TO CELIA'S WAY OF DEALING WITH THE PROBLEM, AND REPEATEDLY TELLS

STORIES ABOUT HERSELF AND OTHER PEOPLE IN ORDER TO ILLUSTRATE THAT HER SOLUTION TO A SIMILAR PROBLEM DESERVES POSITIVE EVALUATION. SHE BEGINS WITH):

Chris: doing it all wrong . doing it all wrong . I used to do that - and people . who . do . ceilings alot and who decorate for other people and who do it professionally say DON'T . GET A ROLLER . PUT IT ON A BROOM HANDLE CLEAR ALL THE FURNITURE OUT THE WAY AND WALK . and you will have the ceiling done within an hour . perfectly . DON'T STAND UP ON LADDERS because the closer you get . the more you can't see what you're doing

Celia: mmm

(* note unelided 'you will')

This pattern continues in a similar way over seventy-two utterances, with Chris issuing direct commands to Celia, frequently punctuating them with short pauses, which gives a staccato effect, and accentuates the feeling that she is giving a list of instructions:

get a roller you'll have it all done in one day

get a roller -- and then the only bit you gotta - are round the edges

and then you do the walls after you've done that --- so you do the walls you can do the walls with a roller

don't mess about with a brush on the ceiling it won't do it as well anyway

always a roller . on a stick . and that's how all professional decorators do it .

you d you don't want to bother with all stuff it's much much quicker if you əm - yeh . that's all you gotta do -- a hole . a broomstick is what you need . definitely ----- and no nonsense

Celia almost invariably responds with very short or minimal acknowledgements, seeming to indicate Chris's superior knowledge in this matter: *mmm*, *yeh*, *oh yeh* *mm* etc.

On only three occasions does Celia try to question Chris, and thus repel the attack, but each occasion is quickly dealt with by Chris, and Celia does not pursue the matter:

1. Celia: well I've been using a roller but . you know I I didn't think I would get the pressure

   Chris: oh you do yeh you do - if you get enough paint on it I mean yeh you get . spatters but *you just cover* everything up

   Celia: *oh*

2. Celia: (....) -- I don't know that the paint actually gets into the edges though does it

   Chris: well it did when she did it

   Celia: ohhh

Chris: but even *if it didn't get*
Celia: *she had the technique*
Chris: right into the edge - you've saved yourself . all that middle . *you've only got*
Celia: *mmm*
3. Chris: (....)if you pay somebody . +they won't get on a ladder+
Celia: +(inaud.)+ the guy that did our lounge . he just stood
Chris: oh he was tall was he (laugh)
Celia: yeh . yes . yes . he was about - about six foot six and . quite long armed for a six foot six man as well and he sort of just went (noise, laugh, gesture)
Chris: oh well that's different for him
Celia: (laugh)
Chris: *but you know that's what everybody does*
Celia: *(inaud.)* he sort of went up about two steps to do the top gutters you know +(laugh)+
Chris: +yeh I know+
Celia: one of those (laugh)
Chris: no it's əm . you d you don't want to bother with all that stuff it's much quicker if you əm - yeh . that's all you gotta do -- a hole . a broomstick
Celia: ahah

Otherwise, the whole sequence consists of Chris telling Celia how wrong she is, and issuing a large number of imperatives, thirteen in the whole sequence.

At the end of this sequence, Chris delivers a short piece of self criticism—very short, considering the length of the preceding attack:

I tell you cause I mean if I can do it absolutely anybody can do it -,

and immediately, in the same utterance, goes on to introduce a new topic, in which both speakers co-operate:

Example (4)
Chris: I thought the old man was supposed to be bringing you today
Celia: noooo
Chris: oh he's collecting you is he
Celia: yes well one of them is . I'm not quite sure which I suggested to Mum that she might like to pass this way on her way home from work and THEY HUMMED AND HAWED AND FIDDLED ABOUT
Chris: ohhh
Celia: because they go out on a Thursday night . and so . INSTEAD OF JUST MAKING ə IT SORT OF NEAT LITTLE DETOUR I said what time'll you be there you know if you're . in hurry to get out you know no problem -- but FOR SOME PECULIAR REASON - the plan - last I heard of it (laugh) was

that DAD WAS GOING TO MAKE A SPECIAL TRIP OVER to collect (inaud.) - which əm

Chris: I DON'T KNOW WHY THEY DO THESE THINGS DON'T ASK ME

Celia: (sigh) WHICH DIDN'T MAKE A LOT OF SENSE BUT THERE WE ARE

Chris: 'S INSANE ISN'T IT --- mind you they have got some shopping for me . she might not want to have it with her at work I suppose

Celia: mmm

Chris: but then why shouldn't she have it with her at work she got it with her at work when she buys it

Celia: yeh

Chris: STUPID (puff) . what time is he coming for you
        (etc.)

In this extract, Chris has originally introduced the new topic, and Celia has converted it from a fairly neutral topic to a suitable Scapegoat, which Celia and Chris collaborate closely to attack over more than seven utterances, three utterances from each speaker being used to present overtly critical opinions of the Scapegoat (see emphasised sections in extract). At the end of the Scapegoat sequence, Chris goes straight on to resume the conversation, and it proceeds with the speakers as equal participants.

It is interesting to note that this repair sequence is much shorter than that used in Example (2)(Dawsons), in section 5.3.5.1, even though the trouble-some sequence is much longer than that in Example (1). This seems to indicate that what is necessary for such a repair is that a suitable (i.e. mutually agreed) Scapegoat should be found, and that both speakers should negatively evaluate that Scapegoat (or specific actions of that Scapegoat)—the length of the repair sequence appears not to be related to the length of the trouble sequence.

Unlike Example (2), this repair is not followed by a topic loop where the conversationalists revert almost immediately to a topic from earlier in the conversation; they do, nevertheless, perform a similar operation over a longer period of time, eventually achieving exactly the same kind of topic loop.

What happens next in this conversation is that the participants spend an unusually long time in Speech-in- action, concerning themselves with topics such as the reason for a third party's absence, what sort of food should be provided for the rest of the day, and what time the meals should be served. This section lasts for thirty-five utterances and is almost exclusively trans-actional, being concerned with what food will actually be cooked that day, and what time it will be served.

The encounter of which this extract is a part is clearly viewed by the participants as primarily an INTERACTION, and the only time at which the speech participants spend any appreciable length of time involved in transaction is the trouble sequence of Example (3) (section 5.3.5.2 above).

This transactional sequence which follows the repair can, I suggest, be seen as in some way balancing or neutralising the trouble of the previous transaction. It can, furthermore, be seen as evidence that the participants have not yet returned to the main purpose of the encounter—the interaction between them; so, although interactive equality may have been restored by the Scapegoat Repair, the speakers have not yet refocused on the interaction, in order to 'test out' the restored equality.

The Story which ends the long transactional sequence finishes with (again) a recompletion:

Celia: but əm -- more or less anything else
Chris: that's QUITE GOOD
Celia: yeh ---
Chris: QUITE GOOD .

and, at this point, Chris initiates a return to 'normal' interaction, by continuing, in the same utterance:

Chris: so which bus did you get on then
Celia: the 733

and this exchange acts as a story slot for the participants to co-operate in exchanging matching evaluations during a lengthy Story element.

Not only is the exchange a way of allowing the participants to begin telling stories again (the preferred method of spoken communication in inter-actions), it also operates as a Topic Loop, because mention of the bus which Celia travelled on has already been made much earlier in the conversation, shortly after the end of the first Story element:

Chris: (....)there's a cat with suspected rabies in Cumberland now *isn't
        there*
Celia: *oh God*
(CELIA PRODUCES BOTTLE OF WINE)
Chris: oh look
Celia: I have brung a bottle
Chris: bzzz
Celia: it's sort of buzzed up a bit it's not really fizzy it's just the way it looks in
        the *bottle (inaud.)*
Chris: *tis now*
Celia: THAT'S THE WAY THE 733 BOUNCES ABOUT (INAUD.)

I have said, in Chapter 4, section 4.3, that Speech-in-action is the main source of new (i.e. unconnected) topics in informal conversation, and the Topic Loop performed by the speakers in this example illustrates this point. On its first mention, the *733 bus* occurs in Speech-in-action, and, like other topics so mentioned, has potential for expansion so that a story can be told as a result of its mention. On this first occasion of mention, this potential is not realised—the speakers do not use the mention to extend into a story, where a variety of new topics may arise. The second mention, however, is fully exploited by the participants so that they can move straight on into Story. This operation can be compared with that described in Chapter 3, section 3.1.1, where a topic from the beginning of an encounter is reinvoked later on. Interestingly, as in the job interviews which provide the exemplification for section 3.1.1, the topic here is also the mode of travel of the incoming speech participant.

It is clear that the Topic Loop which follows the trouble in Example (3) is rather different from that which follows Example (1). There is yet another variation, and all three types will be discussed in the summary to this chapter, after the following sections, which will illustrate and discuss one more instance of repair work in interaction.

5.3.5.3 *Evaluation conflict*

(This extract, although lengthy, will be quoted with only minor space-saving omissions, so as to facilitate the subsequent detailed discussion of the strategies used by the 'offender'.)

Example (5) Tape—Dresses
  SPEECH-IN-ACTION
C: I've got some stuff to show you
  STORY
  I went and bought this this morning cause my mum said she'd treat me she wants me to do a couple for her she's going to America (inaud.)
K: yeh I've just made one yeh
C: I was rather pleased with that
K: yeh HAVE YOU MADE IT ALREADY
C: no no I've just bought it this morning
K: HAVEN'T YOU GOT THE STRAPS
C: come off the bottom
K: oh WHICH ONE D'YOU GET IT ON
C: I got it on the one opposite Woolworth's
K: yeh yeh if you get it from the other one he gives you the straps as well
C: yeh but that other one wasn't there today I saw it Wednesday
K: oh mind you I've just made one and I don't need the straps
C: well I mean look how much
K: yeh
C: see there's tons
K: I know they're ever so good
C: I'm ever so pleased

K: yeh I made one for Shirley and one for me and Shirley doesn't it's a bit too small I didn't quite have enough material four ninety nine

C: four four ninety

K: oh well mine was four *ninety*

C: *yeh* yeh

K: and +nine p+

C: +yeh+

K: for the *straps*

C: *yeh*

K: there you are

C: I was really pleased

K: mmm

C: I was going to get one of the prints but the plain black good good

K: yeh I've just got əm ə it's a white background with lots of stripes on it I only worn it -- what once because I've never had anything like that before and I . I'm all the time . going like this at the moment you know

C: you'll get used to it everybody else is wearing them

K: but əm yeh the the only thing I don't know HAVE YOU WORN THEM BEFORE --

C: WHAT WITH THE STRAPS

K: no like that with it . gathered over the bust . like that

C: (inaud.) some years ago . WHAT ITCHY

K: no it's not itchy but don't YOU'LL LOOK AT YOURSELF IN THE MIRROR AND YOU'LL THINK GOD I LOOK FAT

C: oh

It is clear, just from this extract, that potential trouble has arisen here between the interactants. K has chosen to provide, not positive evaluations which match those provided by C, but to withhold them, and give, instead, a series of minimal acknowledgements (*yeh*, *mm*). She has also introduced a number of questions into the sequence, and it is this strategy which illustrates the connection between the interactional troubles and repairs which are under discussion here and the practical troubles and repairs described by Jefferson, and summarised in section 5.1.1 above.

These questions commence very near the beginning of the sequence, with:

have you made it already,

and the delivery of each of these early questions (which, in all cases, appears to signal a practical trouble, something which requires clarification) serves to defer the point at which K might otherwise be expected to deliver a positive, matching evaluation.

After the questions, K still withholds a positive evaluation and, instead, introduces a new sub-topic—her own dress—which she grants both negative and positive evaluation.

Next, comes another series of apparently 'practical' questions, and these questions, and their answers, form a tightly knit sub-sequence of their own:

> have you worn them before
> what with the straps
> no like that (....) gathered over the bust like that
> some years ago . what itchy
> no (...) but (...) you'll think God I look fat

This short extract shows how a speaker may manipulate the taken-for-granted rules concerning turn-taking and clarification, which govern this kind of side sequence, in order to criticise the hearer (that criticism being the cause of interactive trouble).

A question has, as its inevitable second part, an answer, so every question delivered by K demands an answer by C. The first question she asks in this sequence occurs in an utterance which also contains the words:

> the only thing.

This, in such a context, is a clear signal of a negative evaluation of some kind—in other words, a problem; and it seems that this idea of problem is central to K's linguistic activity in the whole extract. She is refusing to go along with C's attempt to share the telling of a story littered with positive evaluations from both speakers; instead, she is redefining C's story as a problem.

The asking of this first question in the series is, then, for the hearer, closely connected with some kind of problem. She does not, and cannot, know what the problem is, because the question gives no clue—it merely asks the question *have you worn them before*, and this must be answered before the conversation can proceed. Because the hearer has no clue as to what the problem might be, she is forced to guess in order to narrow down the possibilities:

> what with the straps.

This, then, really is a practical trouble; C cannot understand where the conversation is going without further information. The answer to her question still does not cast sufficient light in order to allow the topic to continue:

> no (. . .) gathered over the bust . like that.

Again, K has given insufficient information to allow her to see what might be coming, and so she is under some pressure to give another guess and ask another question:

> what itchy.

At this point, the speakers have been involved in the sub-sequence for four utterances, and, in each of her turns, C has asked a question. The answer she now receives:

(. . .) you'll think God I look fat

is clearly the point to which K has been working from the beginning of the
sub-sequence. This is such a negatively loaded evaluation that it is almost
certain to cause interactional trouble and is, therefore, the kind of 'offence'
rarely to be found in conversation. I suggest that it is allowed to occur here
only because of the prior work put in by K, in the way in which she exploits
the format of practical repairs in order to reach this point, where, after two
questions, C can clearly be seen to have 'asked for it'.

The speakers continue with the topic for a further twenty-six utterances,
still without positive evaluation from K, who, at a later point, also uses direct
imperatives:

make your straps and
well get rid of them,

but this tactic and its relationship to interactional trouble has already been
discussed in detail in section 5.3.5.2. above.

Immediately after this last imperative, the troublesome sequence ends
with:

C: oh (laugh) that's a point - that's a point.

5.3.5.4.1 *Interactive trouble without a Scapegoat Repair*

It would appear, from the other examples discussed in sections 5.3.5.1 and
5.3.5.2 above, that after a lengthy interactional trouble such as this, the
speakers would immediately provide a suitable slot for a Scapegoat Repair.
They do not, however, in this case, perform such a repair, and this gives rise to
two questions: (1) why don't they? and (2) what do they do instead?

As to the reason why no Scapegoat Repair is performed, it appears that the
difference between this trouble and the others is that this one ends with a
recompletion:

oh (laugh) that's a point - that's a point

which is, typically, a topic-terminating device, used by a speaker to signal that
he/she is unable or unwilling to say any more on the current topic. It
therefore puts considerable pressure on the next speaker not to say anything
more on the topic either.

Furthermore, this particular recompletion has two additional characteristics which are also associated with ending topics. Firstly, the utterance in
which C (who has suffered the 'offence') performs the recompletion, begins
with:

oh (laugh).

This laugh is not the latest in a series of laughs, and the interactants are not
involved in a humorous piece of conversation. The laugh in this utterance,

accompanying, as it does, a recompletion, is also signalling the speaker's wish to end the current topic; as Jefferson (in Sudnow 1972: 300) says: [a laugh is an element which is] 'regularly associated with termination of talk.' Secondly, the last part of the recompletion (i.e. the second occurrence of *that's a point*) does not follow what Goldberg describes as the usual pattern of recompletions—which is that the second part is uttered with reduced amplitude—almost as though the speaker's interest in the topic is audibly dying away. In this case, the second part is not uttered with reduced amplitude—instead, C not only increases amplitude, she also artificially lowers the pitch of her voice, so as to produce a very theatrical sound, and uses a very exaggerated intonation pattern thus:

that's a point.

These tactics combine to give the utterance a mocking effect, and, as K's criticisms have been delivered as serious pieces of information, mockery is a clear signal that C does not wish to continue the topic.

I have said, in section 5.3.4 above, that Scapegoat repairs are performed so that participants do not have to acknowledge overtly that interactional trouble has arisen—these repairs redirect the attention of the participants away from the current encounter, and the trouble within it, to negative evaluation of a person who is outside the encounter. The case of Example (5), ending as it does with an emphatic recompletion, is on the boundary between overtly and covertly acknowledged trouble. The use of the recompletion can be seen as a 'hint' that trouble has been noticed, although it is not so explicit that it can be categorised as an overt acknowledgement of that trouble. The speaker here has signalled acknowledgement of trouble sufficiently to have passed the suitable time for a Scapegoat repair. So the speakers do not perform a repair, and this brings me to consideration of my second question—what do the interactants in a case like this do next?

The conversation immediately after the recompletion proceeds like this:

K: so I was a bit disappointed this morning I was gonna have all that skirting
    board painted before I came this morning
C: (inaud.)
K: never mind I bought I put (.....) nineteen trees in my garden this week.

The effectiveness of C's recompletion can now be clearly seen as, immediately following it, K produces a completely different topic. It is also clear from reading the whole transcript, that K feels compelled to produce a new topic QUICKLY—anything to get away from the topic of the troublesome dress—because her 'new' topic is, in fact, one which has already been dealt with at length at the beginning of the conversation; in other words, K has performed (as did the 'offenders' in the other examples) a topic loop, reverting back to an old topic which proceeded without trouble at a time before the trouble arose.

The 'new' topic is not, however, successful, because C's reply is inaudible, which appears to indicate an unwillingness to discuss this topic again. K is then in a position where she has to think of another new topic, and does this by using *never mind* as a link between her disappointment over the paint, and a story about planting some trees (in which she has been successful).

The *tree* topic proceeds for some considerable time, although, in its early stages, it is clear that the trouble from the previous sequence is not forgotten, as C does deliver a number of negative evaluations, aimed at showing that K has planted too many trees. K quickly disposes of C's criticisms, however, and both speakers then collaborate to discuss the trees, and the need for them, over a long sequence. Evaluations are matched throughout, and it appears that the speakers have restored equality of status to the encounter.

There is, however, a further development in the conversation, which shows that unrepaired troubles are not quite so easily forgotten. The *tree* sequence is a lengthy one, and this is followed by four further topics, the last two of which are also very lengthy. In other words, a considerable amount of time elapses (some fifteen minutes approximately), and the conversation has progressed a long way (topically speaking) from the interactional trouble about C's dress. At this point, K REINTRODUCES the topic of the dress. The speakers are discussing C's new earrings:

Example (6)
    SPEECH-IN-ACTION
K: you should have bought some black ones to go with your (GESTURES TOWARDS DRESS LENGTH)
C: well no I couldn't see any nice black shape

(FOUR MORE UTTERANCES CONCERNING THE SHAPE OF EARRINGS, THEN THE CONVERSATION PROCEEDS FOR SEVEN-TEEN UTTERANCES WITH THE SPEAKERS AGAIN DISCUSSING THE DRESS LENGTHS WITHOUT DEVELOPING ANY INTER-ACTIONAL TROUBLE, UNTIL):

K: yes I like that I must admit.

This was, of course, what was wanted by C in her first introduction of the topic—a positive evaluation, to match her own—but it is not delivered until now. After this, the speakers continue to discuss the topic without trouble.

5.3.5.4.2 *Delayed repair*
The reintroduction of the originally troublesome topic (by the original offender) and its positive evaluation by that offender seem to suggest that an unrepaired trouble is not forgotten because the speakers eventually agree to discuss another topic—it is simply laid aside, intact—until, at a later point in the interaction, it can be successfully fitted to some prior topic, and the

trouble can be erased, as in this example by the offender giving a positive, instead of a negative, evaluation.

There is some further evidence (apart from the positive evaluation contrasting with the earlier, negative evaluations) in this conversation that the speakers are, in some way, 'deliberately' retracing their earlier steps in order to get rid of the trouble between them. This evidence is to be found in some 'side' information which is exchanged in both the dress sequences.

When C first introduces the topic, she says:

I've got some stuff to show you I went and bought this this morning cause my mum said she'd treat me she wants me to do a couple for her SHE'S GOING TO AMERICA.

The emphasised clause is clearly audible on the tape, but K ignores it.

In the second occurrence of the topic—BEFORE K delivers her positive evaluation—C says:

well I saw those əm on Wednesday when I was up there and then my mother phoned me up and said oh I want to get a couple of these lengths which I've seen in Watford cause she's going to America in a couple of weeks time

to which K replies:

oh they're going,

C answers:

oh yes,

and K comments:

good for them.

This shows that there is clearly a complete retake of the whole topic—yet another topic loop—even the side sequence of *mum* going to America is rerun; and, interestingly, whereas K ignored this the first time round, she takes the opportunity on the second occasion to show solidarity with C by giving it not only an acknowledgement, but a positive evaluation. So both speakers are collaborating to redo the topic of dress lengths, and this time to do it as equals, showing mutual support and solidarity.

5.4 Scapegoat Repairs in the London–Lund Corpus.

The examples used in sections 5.3.5.1–5.3.5.4.2 above are all taken from my own corpus of conversational material. As section 0.4 in the Introduction to this work makes clear, these conversations involve only a small number of speakers in total, some of whom (including myself) can be heard in more than one of the tapes which make up the corpus. The occurrences of covertly acknowledged interactional trouble, consequent Scapegoat Repairs and Topic Loops are not, however, idiosyncracies of these tapes and this corpus alone, but can, on occasions, be found in any corpus of casual conversation between equals. I do not mean to suggest by this that such discoursal events and manoeuvres will necessarily be found in every such conversation—not all chats involve interactional trouble (or, indeed, practical trouble) between the speakers. The pattern of interactional trouble–Scapegoat Repair–Topic Loop, exemplified and discussed with reference to my own corpus is, however, one which is relevant to chats in general. Two examples of similar structures in conversations from the London–Lund Corpus will show that this claim is justified.

(For full transcriptions of the following examples, refer to Svartvik and Quirk 1980, page numbers given with each example.)

Example (7) London–Lund Corpus. Tape—S.2.4. (463–84)
(p. 463):
d: [m] so you might put her in the picture as regards your occupation
(p. 478) INTERACTIONAL TROUBLE IN THE FORM OF SARCASTIC
         ATTACKS UPON SPEAKER A BY B AND d:
d: how do they respond to your blandishments -
B: (- laughs) they slap his face
c: (. laughs)
A: I don't blandish .
ALL: (--- laugh)
d: you're you're an awkward customer aren't you
A: (--- laughs) - [ʃːm] --- well OK really - I mean ---
d: well what have you told em about *general linguistics for heaven's
        sake*
c,B: *(--- laugh)*
A: very little because there's very little opportunity for doing anything
        except in private conversation .
d: yeah
B: what do you do with them when you're privately conversing

Clearly, the remarks made by B and d are extremely face-threatening to A, because he is being held up as a figure of fun for the amusement of the other participants. This is similar in some ways to Example (1) in section 5.3.5.1 above, where Mary, the child, is discussed as though she is an object, although in this example, most of the face-threatening remarks are addressed to the victim. The effect is, however, similar to that in Example (1), as the 'attacking' utterances seek to rob the victim of all status in the encounter. This can, then, be regarded as another example of the kind of interactional trouble I have already categorised as 'Depersonification'.

The victim in this particular trouble begins to deal with the situation by answering the taunting questions as though they were seriously intended, thus ignoring the threat to his face. After only ten utterances, however, he produces a Scapegoat:

(p. 479):

A: literally last term was riven by this fool of a man - mucking the place up . so that instead of talking [?ə] either reading or Psychology or . Applied Linguistics or anything - all we all we [m] talked was [?ʃm] -- grouses and embitterment +about+

d: +who was this+

B: *Morgan*

A: how bloody *the place* was you see (ETC.)

and (p. 480):

A: well you see he left this . silly man to coordinate

d: who -

A: [ə:] the man who wanted to open all our letters

B: he's not splitting is he

c: oh

d: oh I see

B: (-- laughs) - .

d: yeah -

A: (- laughs)

d: and he doesn't - *coordinate*

B: *coordinate*

B,c: +(-- laugh)+

A: *he's [in]* he's in+capable+ - he's incapable I mean **his

B: **but doesn't he even steer you a little**

A: mind can** . his mind can rise about as high as [ei] roster - and there it just stops -

B: (- laughs)

d: [ə] the [di] this chap is an academic -

A: he wasn't until he came to the unit

d: [m]

A: and he hasn't changed *since*

VAR: *(--- laugh)*

At this point speaker B provides what can be seen as a matching Scapegoat:

(p. 480):

B: sounds like my professor

of whom he says:

B: (....)one would think given his audience that he would be a little - better than - exceedingly elementary (ETC.)

and (p.481):

B: oh yes . he took his first degree . in necromancy *- then he became a
      missionary (- giggles)* then he took his
c: *(--- laughs)*
B: PhD in Linguistics and got a professorship -
c: oh gad
d: so there's hope you see -

The conversation then proceeds with further mockery of speaker A, which is,
this time, less face-threatening, because A joins in and provides some of the
joking comments (see p. 483, LLC). After this, the speakers perform a Topic
Loop:

(p. 484):
d: well how when did you start this process in the first place I mean how did
    you come to become a linguist --

which is a reinvocation (with a slightly different emphasis) of d's comment on
p. 463 (quoted at the beginning of this example) referring to A's occupation.

Example (8) London–Lund Corpus. Tape—S.1.1. (44–8)
(p. 44):
B: [m] -- I've got a problem for you my lad --
A: a problem
B: yes
A: I'm at your service (ETC.)
B: it's not worth . the trouble -- how do you analyse - worth . it's not worth the
    trouble --- (ETC.)

This, beginning as it does with:

I've got a problem for you my lad

is clearly designed by speaker B to be either an academic discussion between
equals on how to analyse *worth*, or, perhaps, a puzzle to which he (B) already
knows the answer, and with which he intends to test A's wits and knowledge.
This is not, however, how the ensuing discussion develops. Instead, speaker A
adopts a role more suitable to a tutor (see Examples (17–22) taken from
tutorial tape 'Julie' in Chapter 3). He does this by going into what might be
thought of as 'teaching mode'. The tactics he uses by which this teaching
mode can be recognised are identical with two of those used by teachers and
described by Sinclair and Coulthard (1975) in their analysis of classroom
discourse:

Evaluate (p. 45):
A: (....)the whole point here is worth . isn't it

B: that's the [w] that's the word he's *after yes*
A: *yes . exactly*

Check (pp. 45–6):
A: (....)you can't say . that . worth . is . adjectival - right
and:
A: (....)it's for five pounds . right
and:
A: (....)it . measures five pounds . right .

(N.B. The three occurrences of *right* all, according to LLC, have rising intonation, which confirms that they are intended to be interpreted as 'checks'.)

In addition, A's utterances throughout this sequence contain instances of statements accompanied by *you see*:

(p. 45):
you see . [əm] . you can't say . that . worth . is . adjectival

which means that it is sui generis you see

(p. 46):
but you see it is sui generis so it'll so . anybody who is looking for [ə:m] . a a niche to fit it a ready-made niche . in English grammar to fit it . into . is sort of begging for the moon -- you see.

These extracts show that speaker A clearly adopts a teaching (and therefore superior) role here; this automatically casts speaker B into an inferior role, which is very different from the role B adopts for himself at the introduction of this topic:

> I've got a problem for you my lad,

and the change in the status balance of the encounter leaves the participants in a state of potential interactional trouble. That the potential trouble is seen as actual trouble by the speakers becomes clear through an examination of how the conversation proceeds.

The topic is brought to a close thus:

(p. 47):
B: it does spot fill definitely as you say with words such as like probably better than with anything else
A: [hm] -- quite so --- [ə:] how many people have you got for the you know if you incidentally we haven't seen each other since that [ə:m] . peculiar meeting with the - [ə:m] -- language - lecturers . remember.

Speaker A's use of the adjective *peculiar* is a signal that this utterance could be introducing a Scapegoat, and the rest of the text shows that B does in fact accept it as such. Both speakers then proceed negatively to evaluate people who were present at the *peculiar meeting*:

(p. 47):
I get rather fed up of some of these youngsters and the claptrap they talk sometimes
God damnation . I'll crown that bastard *before I'm finished with him

(p. 48):
I mean he takes over the whole bloody thing
he is really God Almighty he knows everything
if I don't crown the bastard
almost cross-eyed with those great glasses of his
he certainly has a . hell of a high opinion of himself.

As the Scapegoat sequence finishes, speaker B introduces a new topic:

(p. 48):
there's another - fight I've got on my hands at the moment and you're going to be involved in it before long

and both speakers move straight on to discuss the details of question papers for forthcoming academic examinations—now on equal terms. This new topic is, in fact, a Topic Loop, as this topic has already been discussed earlier in the conversation (see Svartvik and Quirk 1980: 34). The pattern of interactional trouble–Scapegoat Repair–Topic Loop is thus complete. Similar structures, involving interactional trouble of various kinds, followed by Scapegoat Repairs and Topic Loops can be found throughout the London–Lund Corpus—see in particular Tapes S.1.3 (pp. 86–100), S.1.6 (pp. 156–60) and S.2.7 (pp. 545–6). Examples of interactional trouble followed by Scapegoat Repair can also be found in S.1.2 (pp. 80–2), and S.2.3 (pp. 451–61), but these cases do not involve a Topic Loop. Both examples are, however, EXTRACTS from conversations, which clearly end while the conversation is still in progress. The evidence in all the other examples quoted indicates that a Topic Loop can be predicted.

5.5 Negative evaluation unconnected with repairs

Scapegoat Repairs are not the only occasion for negative evaluation of people not present at the encounter, and it should not be assumed that every case of negative evaluation of absent people follows some kind of trouble. There are two other types of negative evaluation sequences, where the person being criticised is clearly not being used as a Scapegoat, the first is where the sequence consists of one speaker presenting the information to another speaker as 'news', in which the hearer acknowledges the information, but does not actually contribute any evaluation. An example of such a sequence can be found later in the 'Dresses' tape:

Example (9) Tape—Dresses
    STORY
K: poor old Arthur
C: what's the matter
K: oh nothing it's . you know all this trouble they had at the office (inaud.) don't you
C: oh with this bloke down in the
K: yeh
C: in the whatsername . yeh
K: yeh . well it's all əm
C: oh not again
K: well no . no no no no . it's not - but - you know the . how that started how he kept saying that they weren't pulling up . our end *weren't pulling*
C: *oh yeh*
K: their weight and all the rest of it . well I think I said to you at the time Arthur was terribly upset because m . Martin had made it sound as though it was əm . him and Ernie
C: yeh
K: not pulling their weight . whereas in actual fact . Helen -
C: oh yes you said there was somebody else
K: and Henry - Henry's going ---
C: where to --
K: well -- there are . be k (gasp, laugh) thi . it . you know when you have a partnership you have this contractual agreement that if anyone leaves the partnership . they're not allowed to . practise within . so many miles of the
    .
C: I didn't realise that but that sounds fairly reasonable *yeh*
K: *yeh*
C: like hairdressers and people
K: that's right . not allowed to .
C: yeh
K: and they're not allowed to take more than a p certain percentage of the
C: *yeh*
K: *clients* with them or what have you . well the (gasp) poor old ha Henry . he's so inefficient and .
    SPEECH-IN-ACTION
    you having trouble with that
C: yeh . I always do with these
    STORY

K: he's so inefficient and all this anyway he's going and they're letting him .
     start up a practice just down the road
C: you're kidding
K: no . Arthur said he's so bloody inefficient it'll only be there six months
C: oh . yeh . they're not worried -
     SPEECH-IN-ACTION
K: əm you're making your ear ever so sore look
     (ETC.)

In this example, only speaker K (the story teller) gives the negative evaluations, while speaker C, apart from minimal acknowledgements (*yeh*), simply provides first a comment, signalling acknowledgement of, and encouragement for the speaker's evaluation:

                    you're kidding,

and then a comment summing up the situation as presented by the speaker, and signalling understanding:

              oh . yeh . they're not worried.

At no time does this hearer provide an evaluation to match, or contrast with, the speaker's evaluation, and this lack of substantial contribution by the hearer cannot be explained by her ignorance of the efficiency (or otherwise) of the person who is under discussion. As Chapter 4 shows, whether or not a speaker contributes substantially to a story is a matter of choice, not background knowledge, and where there is little or no background knowledge, a guess will suffice. The presentation of the negative evaluation sequence in this story by one speaker only marks that sequence as NEWS, given by one speaker to another. This distinguishes it from the Scapegoat Repair sequence, where the negative evaluation is essentially SHARED by both speakers.

The second type of negative sequence which is unconnected with Scapegoat Repairs occurs where both parties contribute evaluations, but the negative component is balanced by positive evaluations of the person under discussion. An example of this occurs in the 'Celia' tape, but as it is an unusually long sequence (approximately seventeen minutes) I will only provide extracts from it here. The two speakers are negatively evaluating a third person, and B is describing a porch built by this person:

Example (10) Tape—Celia
Chris: it's incredible this porch it's just a joke . and in every other way he's so .
     clever inside the house you can see what he's done (etc.)(..) it's
     amazing (..)you know he does things like and he's really brilliant with
     wood . and this porch . ohhh George *(laugh)*
Celia: *(laugh)*

Chris: 's a disaster (etc.) crazy . you know normally he's so brilliant with
      things like that but . ohhh +dear+
Celia: +brilliant+ with doing but obviously the taste is somewhat awry

Throughout this topic, although Chris is providing most of the information, both speakers contribute evaluations, many of which are negative. Balancing these, however, there are positive evaluations of the person under discussion, so, although George's porch is described as *a disaster*, his other woodwork is described as *brilliant*, and, although this latest work shows that his *taste is somewhat awry*, he is still *so . clever inside the house*, where he has done work which is *amazing*.

This balancing of evaluations distinguishes a sequence of this kind from a Scapegoat sequence, because any individual being used as a Scapegoat suffers ONLY negative evaluations from both speaker and hearer; and, in addition to this, an evaluation sequence such as this is further distinguishable from a Scapegoat Repair by the absence of a Topic Loop.

5.6 Summary and comments

It is clear, from the preceding exemplification and discussion, that co-conversationalists telling stories about absent people can negatively evaluate those absent people in several ways, and, whichever way this is done, collaboration and agreement in the evaluation strengthens the interactive unity of the speakers.

Using an absent person as a Scapegoat, however, is a rather special kind of story, employing only negative evaluations. It is characterised by substantial contributions from both speakers in the interaction (repeated contributions of *mm* are not substantial contributions—they are minimal acknowledgements which merely allow the other speaker to continue), and by the absence of any positive evaluation which may balance the negative aspect. It is to be found in conversation after interactional trouble between the participants, that trouble arising from the occurrence of an imbalance in the status differential between the speakers.

The function of a Scapegoat Repair is to allow the interactants, who have, as a result of the preceding trouble, been on opposite sides of a status boundary, to present themselves as on the same side, against an absent Scapegoat, so that equality can be restored to the current interaction.

The repair workings which follow interactional trouble often involve Scapegoat Repairs, but this is not always so. Interactional trouble is, however, ALWAYS followed by some kind of topic movement, either following the repair itself, or, if the trouble is unrepaired, a rerun of the initially troublesome topic in order to erase the trouble from it. The major topic movements associated with interactional troubles are Topic Loops, involving a return by the speakers to topics already discussed earlier in the encounter.

Interactional trouble is, then, one of the causes of major topic disruption and movement in dialogue; when once it has occurred, it can be predicted that a topic move BACKWARDS will follow. In addition to this, a secondary kind of predictability can also be found in this kind of structuring—this is the predictability which arises from the presence in the conversation of the extreme kind of negative evaluation of an absent party which characterises a Scapegoat Repair; if such evaluation is present then it follows that interactive trouble MUST have occurred earlier in the same conversation.

Scapegoat Repairs and Topic Loops are, then, major factors in the topical construction of informal, relaxed conversation, and their existence, which has been demonstrated throughout this chapter, is evidence for what has, until now, been unrecognised—an ongoing monitoring and planning of the topics of so-called 'spontaneous' conversation.

6 Conclusions

6.1 Summary and comments

The preceding chapters have dealt with the interpersonal aspect of spoken communication in terms of what I have shown to be its fundamental component—relative speaker status. The interpersonal workings of primarily transactional encounters have been discussed in Chapter 3 with special reference to interviews and a tutorial, and Chapters 4 and 5 have dealt in detail with the management and progression of interactional encounters, i.e. those which have the interpersonal aspect as their main focus.

It has been shown throughout my discussion that relative speaker status is, in fact, the basis on which each encounter depends—first for definition and second for the management of topical progression.

Transactional encounters, which arise out of, and reflect institutions in the society, depend for their definition on fixed status—that is, official status in the institutions which exist independently of the encounter—in that speech participants adopt a particular set of complementary roles which are not only suitable, but obligatory for the particular encounter type. These roles have two aspects: firstly, they are actual instances of particular kinds of institutional roles, e.g. teacher, doctor, interviewer; secondly (and dependently), they have a particular status orientation—in the case of doctor, teacher, interviewer this would be SUPERIOR, and in the case of patient, pupil, interviewee it would be INFERIOR.

Any such role adopted by a speaker is, of course, only valid if it forms a part of a complementary set such as doctor/patient, or interviewer/interviewee, such sets being concrete instances of the underlying status pattern of superior/inferior. The adoption of any such role is not a matter for a unilateral decision—it requires the consent and co-operation of speakers on both sides to validate one another's roles and thereby define the encounter type. The precise terms of this consent and co-operation are, in the case of primarily transactional encounters, established and fixed at the outset of the encounter (in practice, usually prior to the encounter), and those terms (i.e. who is the interviewer (superior) and who the interviewee (inferior)) remain constant throughout; they are not, under any circumstances, renegotiable at any point IF THE ENCOUNTER TYPE IS TO BE PRESERVED; any renegotiation of roles will automatically redefine the encounter.

In the same way that each transaction is constrained by a particular role-patterning, so it is similarly constrained by a particular set of appropriate and permitted conversational topics which are relevant to the particular institution which is encoded in the transaction. These topics are also related to relative speaker status, in that they are accessible to the speech participants in assymmetrical ways. In an interview, for example, a permitted, acceptable (and, indeed, obligatory) topic would be the educational background and previous work experience of the interviewee, and the permitted, acceptable, obligatory raiser of this topic is the interviewer. The roles with regard to this topic are not interchangeable, it must be oriented by the superior towards the inferior participant—the interviewee is not permitted to raise a similar topic oriented towards the interviewer's history. The superior speaker in such an encounter is not, of course, permitted to raise simply any topic—he/she is constrained only to those topics which can be seen as relevant to the current transaction.

Speakers in transactions are governed by strict rules in terms of their relative status, the roles they may adopt within the limitations of the status appropriate to the encounter, the range of permitted conversational topics, and the responsibility for introducing those topics.

These observations have, of course, been made by a number of other writers—e.g. Lacoste (1981) in a discussion of medical consultations, and Thomas (1985) in a discussion of disciplinary police interviews—and the importance of status in unequal, transactional encounters is well established (though only implied) in the writings of many sociolinguists (e.g. Fishman (1971) and Denison (1971) in their studies of bilingualism). What has not, until now, been fully appreciated, is that interactional encounters between equals are also dependent for their definition and management on relative speaker status.

Like transactions, interactions encode certain aspects and patterns of the culture in which they occur, but, unlike transactions, these aspects of the culture are not (in English at least) so unambiguously recognisable as to warrant a unique reference in the language. Whereas a transaction between a doctor and a patient can be unambiguously and uncontroversially referred to as a 'medical consultation', a transaction between a potential employer/ employee can similarly be referred to as a 'job interview', and a transaction between a tutor and a student can be referred to as a 'tutorial', there is no unique reference term for the kind of conversational exchange which I have, throughout this work, called an 'interactional encounter'. Similarly, the participants of an interactional encounter cannot be uniquely identified in the language—they are not doctors, students, patients, they are just people. We can say, then, that while interactional encounters do encode certain aspects of the culture, there is no clear cut cultural INSTITUTION (in the 'official' sense of the word) which they encode, and, consequently, no institutional role types open to the speakers. This itself is, however, one way in which an interaction is defined, in that the participants in an interaction are constrained NOT to adopt institutionalised roles such as teacher, doctor, interviewer. Similarly, they are constrained not to adopt any role which carries with it a CONSTANT superior or inferior orientation; the creation of an interaction is dependent on the avoidance of such roles and the preservation of speaker equality through an even EXCHANGE of roles.

Whereas the interpersonal balance of a transaction is fixed at the outset, an interaction has no such pre-arranged pattern; instead, its balance must be negotiated and re-negotiated throughout the course of the encounter. As the bulk of interaction takes place through the medium of speech, the inter-personal workings involving the constant re-negotiation of roles are most clearly observed in the linguistic interchange over the whole of the discourse. The model described in Chapter 4 reveals the way in which this interpersonal monitoring takes place; speakers spend the bulk of interaction in Story, which, in the dialogic form in which it generally occurs in interaction, provides an ideal medium for the preservation of equality through a constant exchange of roles. Throughout Story, the continual manipulation of the practical rules of dialogue result in generally very short conversational turns in which both speech participants exchange roles of superior and inferior in the areas of topic introduction, topic shift and questioning. Throughout these sequences, speaker solidarity is created and expressed by the frequent uttering of matching evaluations of various aspects of the stories in focus. The building of the interpersonal structure of interaction is, then, intimately linked to the practical creation of the text.

I have argued in the Introduction to this work, section 0.2., that the overall goal of an interaction is the creation and maintenance of interpersonal ties between the speech participants, so the sequences which carry these inter-personal messages (dialogic stories, matching evaluations, etc.) are not simply sections which function to facilitate or progress the text—they are, rather, the mainspring of the text. The interpersonal strand is, in fact, the major factor in the creation of the textual strand.

This gives the stories (etc.) a rather different status from the purely interactional phases which occur during transactional encounters, which (by establishing and maintaining status DIFFERENCES between the participants) function primarily to help define and maintain the character of the encounter, and also to (in a sense) fill in gaps between transactional sections and thereby help to facilitate and progress the ongoing transaction.

Interactions do not have an equivalent two-tier structure of 'main business' and 'subsidiary interaction'; the examples used throughout this work do, however, illustrate an overwhelming tendency in all the interactive data inspected for speakers in interaction to spend most of their time involved in Story and to interrupt these lengthy sections of Story only briefly by phases of Speech-in-action (many of which are transactional in nature).

Speakers use Speech-in-action at what appear to be topical boundaries in the encounter, i.e. the beginning and the end of the encounter and between occurrences of Story which do not have a clear topical link. When Speech-in-action is used it often serves to effect a transaction which is, in a sense, both subsidiary to the ongoing interaction (in that it can be regarded as a 'side issue'), and also an integral part of that interaction (in that it is embedded in activities whose cultural significance is so tied to interaction that those activities are seen as typical in an interactional context). An example of this would be the offering and acceptance of food or drink during an informal chat. Although a phase of Speech-in-action dealing with such a transaction would be, in one way, subsidiary to the chat, its presence in a chat is so typical that (the physical environment of the encounter permitting) its absence in a chat of any duration (say thirty minutes or so) could be regarded as abnormal, or at least unusual.

This viewing of Speech-in-action and Story as a relationship of subsidiary and main passages of interaction can, at one level, be equated with the subsidiary and main levels observable in transaction; i.e. transactions have brief, subsidiary interludes of interaction which help to further the ultimate transactional goal of the encounter, and interactions have brief, subsidiary interludes of transaction which help to further the ultimate interactional goal of the encounter. However, the close embedding in interaction of the transactions which typically occur during Speech-in-action, the importance of those (apparently trivial) transactions to the preservation of friendly interpersonal relationships, and a brief reconsideration of the overall purpose of interaction (i.e. the forming and development of interpersonal relationships) provide the justification for regarding BOTH Speech-in-action and Story as essentially composing the mainstream of interaction.

The preceding chapters have shown by discussion and exemplification that the establishment and maintenance of interpersonal relationships through spoken dialogue is most clearly observed and described by considering the status patterns which the speakers create and monitor as the encounter progresses.

The transactional examples discussed in Chapter 3 display the expected constant superior/inferior status signalling throughout, and the analyses in Chapter 5 justify the argument that status is similarly crucial in interactional encounters, by showing that status imbalance occasions meticulous (and sometimes lengthy) repair work by the participants—thus showing that the notion of status as the central factor in the interpersonal strand of interactional encounters is not merely a useful concept for the retrospective analyst, but a reality for the speakers concerned. Relative speaker status can, then, be justifiably regarded as the basis on which interpersonal relationships turn.

I would argue further that status has a hitherto unrecognised importance in terms of the discourse—that is, it is a major factor (possibly the major factor) in the three-way link between the ideational, interpersonal and textual strands of discourse. I have already explained how, in primarily interactional discourse, status can be seen as functioning to cement both the interpersonal and textual strands of discourse. This does not mean, however, that status in interactional discourse can be regarded as simply a subsidiary (albeit essential) thread which serves only to link two major discourse strands, interpersonal and textual. In interaction, the interpersonal strand is paramount, i.e. its preservation and progress is, in an overall sense, the 'reason for' the encounter—so the textual strand is relegated to a subsidiary, dependent position. As the interpersonal strand is based on relative speaker status, it is clear that, in primarily interactional discourse, status is actually the basis on which BOTH the interpersonal and textual strands depend.

Consideration of the association between the ideational strand and relative speaker status reveals a rather different relationship, and a surprising difference between the relationship as it occurs in interactional encounters and as it occurs in transactional encounters.

In interactional encounters, the ideational strand is, of course, subsidiary to the interpersonal strand in one sense, i.e. it is the interpersonal strand which most clearly expresses the overall goal of the encounter. There are, as I have already pointed out (this chapter, p. 119) restrictions on speakers as to how they orient themselves towards the ideational content of what is said, but this orientation is, of course, a matter of INTERPERSONAL, not ideational management. There are, however, very few restrictions on what might constitute the ideational strand, i.e. what conversational topics might be raised. So although, in an overall sense, the ideational strand is subsidiary to the interpersonal strand, its inner constitution is such, in interaction, that it can be regarded as independent of the interpersonal strand, and therefore independent of relative speaker status.

In transactional encounters, however, the situation is very different; the range of possible conversational topics is extremely restricted—they must be directly related to the overall transactional goal—that is, speakers must perceive them as leading towards that goal. Closely associated with the transactional goal (i.e. subsidiary but essential to it) is the relative status of the speakers as realised by the appropriate complementary roles which they enact. Speakers in transactions are, then, strictly constrained to the discoursal pursuit of the transactional goal and equally strictly constrained as to the ideational content, and maintenance of the encounter type is largely dependent on speakers remaining within the confines of their 'fixed status'.

It is clear, then, that in transactions although the transactional goal (and therefore the ideational strand) is paramount, there are very strong links between the ideational and the status-based interpersonal strand—stronger links, in fact, than in the interactional encounters, where there are comparatively few restrictions on ideational content.

We can see, from this argumentation, that the importance of the interpersonal strand in discourse, whether transactional or interactional, has been underestimated; in transactional discourse it is strongly influential in the building of the ideational strand, and in interactional discourse it functions as the basis for the textual strand. The interpersonal strand itself has as its basis relative speaker status, and we can therefore say that status functions as the basis for the transmission of meanings not only at the level of interpersonal communication, but also at the ideational and textual levels, in both transactional and interactional discourse.

6.2 Suggestions for further research

This work has been concerned mainly with giving an interactional overview of the workings of status in transactional and interactional encounters, and showing the resulting importance of the interpersonal strand of communication.

In primarily interactional discourse, the kind of structures which I have exemplified and shown to be interactionally relevant (Story, Speech-in-action, Scapegoats, Topic Loops) are structures which exert a broad influence over large sections of the discourse, and all these areas have potential for further study and research.

Story is a large discourse element which may (and often does) contain several stories which are usually topically linked. Further small-scale analysis within the general category of Story would establish whether there are subdivisions which could be made which would be discoursally relevant, and may throw light on how the various stories which make up the element Story are linked, e.g. whether their arrangement within the element is in any way hierarchical, with, perhaps, the first story in the element having different characteristics from those which follow it.

Speech-in-action could also be the focus for closer study, both in terms of its internal construction (i.e. whether the physical or social aspects of the encounter are talked about), and in the area of the way in which it is linked to instances of Story; it seems likely, for instance, that particular kinds of Speech-in-action will occur adjacent to particular kinds of Story.

This current work has shown that Scapegoat Repairs are used in cases of interactional trouble which occur within primarily interactional encounters. Further research may show that there are other similar structures which are used to distract speakers from particular conversational topics. There may, for instance, be predictable conversational strategies which allow speakers to avoid the unambiguous and acknowledged adoption of potentially troublesome topics altogether—in fact the existence of such strategies seems intuitively highly likely. To establish whether or not this is indeed the case would, however, require a close analysis of a very large corpus of interactional material, as not all interactions (and not all interpersonal relationships) are marked by conversational 'no go' areas.

Associated with repairs I have described a phenomenon which I have termed 'Topic Loop', where speakers may either revert to an interactionally 'safe' topic which has already occurred earlier in the discourse, or, in the absence of a Scapegoat, may reinvoke a previously troublesome topic in order to 'erase' the trouble. Further study in this area may show that only certain topics can be considered by speakers as 'safe'; furthermore, it seems likely that a close analysis of a large corpus of transactional encounters may reveal a large amount of Topic Looping, particularly in transactions such as job interviews, where it may have a different function from that which I have observed, exemplified and described in interactions.

One other possible area of interest for further research arising from this current work would be a detailed analysis of speech encounters which fall into the category of interactional dialogue, but which have other, complicating aspects, the TV chat show being a particularly interesting example of such a discourse type. Such a study would provide excellent opportunities for the analysis of stories told as a monologue, i.e. Malinowski's 'narrative' function of language (see Chapter 1, section 1.3.1).

All these suggestions for further research along the lines which I have outlined would involve a rather 'lower-level' analysis than I have performed in these chapters. My aim in this current work has been to provide a broad view of the interpersonal workings which operate throughout transactional and interactional encounters, to show how the structures and strategies which I have observed in the data operate in the formation and management of the whole discourse, and to provide a clearly exemplified model for further work in the area of face-to-face dialogue.

It is hoped that the overview provided here will be of use in further studies, not only of conversation for its own sake (some suggestions for which I have outlined above), but also in the more immediately practical area of the human/machine interface problem which is so pervasive throughout academic research today. If it is to be of use in this area, then it seems likely that the most initially fruitful direction for further research would be a more detailed clarification of the phenomenon of Stories, particularly taking into consideration their inner structure. As I have shown, it is clear that English speakers regard the Story as the preferred method of spoken communication—particularly when at their most relaxed—so it would seem that a more detailed look at the inner workings of spoken stories would be a good starting point for the improvement of the 'front ends' which are such a vital part of the various expert systems which are currently either in use or under development.

Bibliography

Abercrombie, D. (1956), *Problems and Principles*, London, Longman.

Argyle, M. (1969), *Social Interaction*, London, Tavistock.

—— (1972), *The Psychology of Interpersonal Meaning*, Harmondsworth, Middx., Penguin Books.

Bateson, G., 'Toward a Theory of Schizophrenia', in *Behavioural Science* 1, (1956).

Bellack, A. A. *et al* (1966), *The Language of the Classroom*, Teachers College, Columbia University, New York, Teachers College Press.

Berne, E. (1964), *The Games People Play*, New York, Grove Press.

Brazil, D., Coulthard, M. and Johns, C. (1980), *Discourse Intonation and Language Teaching*, London, Longman.

Buhler, K. (1934), *Sprachtheorie*, Jena, Fisher.

Brown, G. (1977), *Listening to Spoken English*, London, Longman.

Brown, G. and Yule, G. (1983), *Teaching the Spoken Language*, Cambridge, Cambridge University Press.

Brown, R. and Gilman, A. (1960), 'The pronouns of power and solidarity', in Laver, J. and Hutcheson, S. (eds) (1972), *Communication in Face to Face Interaction*, Harmondsworth, Middx., Penguin Books.

Brown R. and Ford, M. (1961), 'Address in American English', in Laver, J. and Hutcheson, S. (eds) (1972), *Communication in Face to Face Interaction*, Harmondsworth, Middx., Penguin Books.

Burton, D. (1980), *Dialogue and Discourse*, London, Routledge and Kegan Paul.

Coulthard, M. and Montgomery, M. (1981), *Studies in Discourse Analysis*, London, Routledge and Kegan Paul.

Crow, B. (1983), in Craig and Tracey (eds) (1983), *Conversational Coherence*, London, Sage.

Crystal, D. and Davey, D. (1969), *Investigating English Style*, London, Longman.

—— (1975), *Advanced Conversational English*, London, Longman.

de Beaugrande, R. (1982), 'The story of grammars and the grammar of stories', *Journal of Pragmatics*, 6, 383–422.

Denison, N. (1971), 'Some observations on language variety and plurilingualism', in Pride, J. B. and Holmes, J. (eds) (1972), *Sociolinguistics*, Harmondsworth, Middx., Penguin Books.

Di Pietro, R. J. (1981), 'The many dimensions of conversational language', in Copeland, J. E. and Davis, P. W. (eds) (1981), *The Seventh Lacus Forum 1980*, Columbia, SC, Hornbeam Press.

Ervin-Tripp, S. (1969), 'Sociolinguistic rules of address', in Pride, J. and Holmes, J. (eds) (1972), *Sociolinguistics*, Harmondsworth, Middx., Penguin Books.

Esau, H. and Poth, A. (1981), 'Dominance patterns in conversational interaction', in Copeland, J. E. and Davis, P. W. (eds) (1981) *The Seventh Lacus Forum 1980*, Columbia, SC, Hornbeam Press.

Fishman, J. A. (1971), 'The relationship between micro- and macro-sociolinguistics in the study of who speaks what language to whom and when', in Pride, J. B. and Holmes, J. (eds) (1972), *Sociolinguistics*, Harmondsworth, Middx., Penguin Books.

Garfinkel, H. (1967), *Studies in Ethnomethodology*, NJ, Prentice-Hall.

Goffman, E. (1955), 'On face work: an analysis of ritual elements in social interaction', in Laver, J. and Hutcheson, S. (eds) (1972), *Communication in Face to Face Interaction*, Harmondsworth, Middx., Penguin Books.

—— (1957), 'Alienation from interaction', in Laver, J. and Hutcheson, S. (eds) (1972), *Communication in Face to Face Interaction*, Harmondsworth, Middx., Penguin Books.

—— (1969), *The Presentation of Self in Everyday Life*, Harmondsworth, Middx., Penguin Books.

—— (1971), *Interaction Ritual*, Harmondsworth, Middx., Penguin Books.

—— (1971), *Relations in Public*, Harmondsworth, Middx., Penguin Books.

—— (1981), *Forms of Talk*, Oxford, Basil Blackwell.

Goldberg, J. A. (1978), 'Amplitude shift: a mechanism for the affiliation of utterances in conversational interaction', in Schenkein, J. (ed.) (1978), *Studies in the Organisation of Conversational Interaction*, New York, Academic Press.

Halliday, M. A. K. (1975), 'Language as social semiotic: towards a general socio-linguistic theory', in Makkai, A. and Makkai, V. B. (eds) *The First Lacus Forum 1974*, Columbia, SC, Hornbeam Press.

Harris, J., Little, D. and Singleton, D. (eds) (1986), *Perspectives on the English Language in Ireland*, Dublin, CLCS/TCD.

Harris, S. (1984), 'Questions as a mode of control in magistrates' courts', *International Journal of the Sociology of Language*, 49, 5–27.

Hayakawa, S. I. (1941), *Language in Thought and Action*, New York, Harcourt Brace Jovanovich.

Jefferson, G. and Schenkein, J. (1977), 'Some sequential negotiations in conversation: unexpanded and expanded versions of projected action sequences', in Schenkein, J. (ed.) (1978), *Studies in the Organisation of Conversational Interaction*, New York, Academic Press.

Labov, W. (1982), *Language in the Inner City, Studies in Black English Vernacular*, Philadelphia, University of Pennsylvania Press.

Lacoste, M. (1981), 'The old woman and the doctor: a contribution to the analysis of unequal linguistic exchanges', *Journal of Pragmatics*, 5, 169–80.

Laver, J. (1975), 'Communicative functions of phatic communion', in Kendon, A., Harris, R. and Key, M. (eds) (1975), *The Organisation of Behaviour in Face to Face Interaction*, The Hague, Mouton.

—— (1981), 'Linguistic routines in greeting and parting', in Coulmas, F. (ed.) (1981), *Conversational Routine*, The Hague, Mouton.

Laver, J. and Hutcheson, S. (eds) (1972), *Communication in Face to Face Interaction*, Harmondsworth, Middx., Penguin Books.

Leech, G. (1974), *Semantics*, Harmondsworth, Middx., Penguin Books.

Leech, G., Deuchar, M. and Hoogeuraad, R. (1982), *English Grammar for Today: A New Introduction*, London, Macmillan.

Lyons, J. (1977), *Semantics, vols. 1 and 2*, Cambridge, Cambridge University Press.

McTear, M. F. (1979), 'Is conversation structured?: towards an analysis of informal spoken discourse', in Wolck, W. and Garvin, P. L. (eds) (1979), *The Fifth Lacus Forum 1977*, Columbia, SC, Hornbeam Press.

Malinowski, B. (1922), *Argonauts of the Western Pacific*, London, Routledge and Kegan Paul.

—— (1923), 'The problem of meaning in primitive languages', in Ogden, C. K. and Richards, I. A. (eds) (1923), *The Meaning of Meaning*, London, Routledge and Kegan Paul.

—— (1923), 'Phatic communion', in Laver, J. and Hutcheson, S. (eds) (1972), *Communication in Face to Face Interaction*, Harmondsworth, Middx., Penguin Books.

—— (1926), *Crime and Custom in Savage Society*, London, Routledge and Kegan Paul.

—— (1929), *The Sexual Life of Savages in N. W. Melanesia*, London, Routledge and Kegan Paul.

Mathiot, M. and Dougherty, E. (1978), 'A functional empiricist approach to the analysis of face to face interaction', in Paradis, M. (ed.) (1978), *The Fourth Lacus Forum 1977*, Columbia, SC, Hornbeam Press.

Monaghan, J. (1979), *The Neo-Firthian Tradition and its Contribution to General Linguistics*, Tübingen, Niemeyer.

Pride, J. B. and Holmes, J. (1972), *Sociolinguistics*, Harmondsworth, Middx., Penguin Books.

Prince, G. (1973), *A Grammar for Stories*, The Hague, Mouton.

Quirk, R. and Greenbaum, S. (1973), *A University Grammar of English*, London, Longman.

Sacks, H., Schegloff, E. and Jefferson, G. (1974), 'A simplest systematics for the organisation of turn taking for conversation', in Schenkein, J. (ed) (1978), *Studies in the Organisation of Conversational Interaction*, New York, Academic Press.

Sacks, H. (1975), 'Everyone has to lie', in Sanches, M. and Blount, B. G. (eds) (1975), *Sociocultural Dimensions of Language Use*, New York, Academic Press.

Schank, R. C. (1977), 'Rules and topics in conversation', *Cognitive Science*, 1, 421–42.

Schegloff, E. A. and Sacks, H. (1973), 'Opening up closings', in Turner, R. (ed.) (1974), *Ethnomethodology*, Harmondsworth, Middx., Penguin Books.

Schenkein, J. (ed.) (1978), *Studies in the Organisation of Conversational Interaction*, New York, Academic Press.

Simpson, P. (1986), 'Phatic communion in Flam O'Brien's *The Third Policeman*', in Harris, J. Little, D. and Singleton, D. (eds) (1986), *Perspectives on the English Language in Ireland*, Dublin. CLCS/TCD.

Sinclair, J.McH. and Coulthard, R. M. (1975), *Towards an Analysis of Discourse*, Oxford, Oxford University Press.

Stein, N. L. (1982), 'The definition of a story', *Journal of Pragmatics*, 6, 487–507.

Stubbs, M. (1976), *Language, Schools and Classrooms*, London, Methuen.

Sudnow, D. (ed.) (1972) *Studies in Social Interaction*, New York, Free Press.

Thomas, J. A. (1985), 'The language of power: towards a dynamic pragmatics', *Journal of Pragmatics*, 9, 765–84.

Turner, G. W. (1973), *Stylistics*, Harmondsworth, Middx., Penguin Books.

Wilson, J. 1985 'Conversation matters: Towards a Theory of Conversation', unpublished Ph.D. thesis, Queens University, Belfast.

Index